D1642287

FOUR WALLS ADORNED

A History of English Costume

English Children's Costume since 1775

English Costume in the Age of Elizabeth

English Costume of the Early Middle Ages

English Costume of the Late Middle Ages

English Costume of the 17th Century

English Costume of the 18th Century (with James Laver)

English Costume of the 19th Century (with James Laver)

Western European Costume, Vol. I

Western European Costume, Vol. II

A History of English Footwear

English Costume, 1900–1950

COMBE, GITTISHAM. DEVON

FOUR WALLS ADORNED

INTERIOR DECORATION 1485–1820

BY

IRIS·BROOKE

METHUEN & CO. LTD.

36, ESSEX STREET, STRAND, LONDON, W.C. 2

First published in 1952

Catalogue No. 3274/U

Printed by Brüder Rosenbaum, Vienna, Austria

TO

HUGH GIFFARD

WILLIAM GAUNT

AND

F. GORDON ROE

FOR THEIR HELP AND ENCOURAGEMENT

CONTENTS

COLOUR PLATES

FOREWORD

Though wars, revolutions, political upheavals, floods and fires, all conspire to the shaping of history, it is not this sort of history in which the great majority of people care to live. In fact these things have usually provoked a natural instinct in human beings to protect themselves from all violent outside disturbances by the aesthetic distraction of their immediate domestic surroundings.

It is this intimate background—the stage on which life is played—that is such an important part of the social history of this, or any other country. In much the same way that clothes reflect the manners of any period, so do the decorations of the four walls which form our daily background.

Ever since the first cave-man was inspired to decorate his walls by cutting or scratching scenes of the hunt on its surface, man has sought to beautify his home by decorating its inside walls with imaginative scenes and design, based on contemporary knowledge, sport, travel or amusements typical of his particular lifetime.

We can in a sense re-live the lives of our remotest human predecessors in reviewing these inside walls or what remains of them.

Each succeeding civilization has left us a wealth of such stories of intimate life from Egyptian and Babylonian reliefs, Greek and Aegean frescoes, Roman and Byzantine mosaics down to the gorgeous wall paintings of Renaissance Italy and the rich tapestries of fifteenth century France.

The aim and scope of this book is, however, limited to the decoration of the inside of English homes from the time of Henry VII to the close of the Regency Period. It is a vast subject and if taken too solidly tends to give one mental indigestion, so I have tried to discard much that is repetitive and sought out the 'bits and pieces' that to my mind are the stepping stones to a fuller knowledge of each phase in the history of our domestic surroundings. Once the general trends in design have been digested, the undated features fall into their rightful place and the whole can be viewed in reasonable perspective.

In order the better to illustrate this I have introduced from time to time, at periods of half a century or so, coloured drawings of rooms peopled and furnished as they might have been within a few years of their completion. They are all 'New Rooms' and probably each in their way were remarkable for their up to date innovations. I doubt if any of the rooms illustrated were inspired by foreign example, in most cases they must have been the work of local or travelling craftsmen, and they are therefore essentially English. With the exception of Chillington and Ramsbury (both chosen for their typical wallpapers) they are all small or medium sized homes.

An interesting feature to remember is that, traditionally, when a bride was brought into an old house one room, at least, was 'done up' for her personal use. Thus we find many charming up-stairs rooms obviously of a period considerably later than the house itself. When such rooms were renovated it was not only the decoration of walls and ceiling that received attention. The whole room was altered to accommodate the new style with windows, doors, door-cases and fireplaces all in keeping with the panelling, plasterwork or wall papers which were being introduced. Such rooms are perfect specimens of the traditional fashion of their time.

The most difficult feature that confronts one in a book on this subject is that of the vicissitudes through which any property has passed during the centuries since it was built; the fortunes that have been lavished on its 'improvements', the fantastic or coldly practical ideas of the various owners of such fortunes; or again their misfortunes—fires, wars, poverty, disrepair et cetera.

Practically every owner has left his mark, and it may be difficult to say exactly at what date such and such a room has been reconstructed. Some features are of course quite easy to date, whilst others present an almost insurmountable problem. At certain late phases of our history there have been those who, delighted with the 'quaintness' of an earlier age have endeavoured to repeat or restore to the best of their knowledge. Frequently such knowledge has been misfounded and the ensuing results are both misleading and confusing. It has, therefore, been my aim to search out features and details that can be given a fairly accurate date, and amongst these I have been fortunate enough to find some superb examples of craftsmanship that have remained untouched since the day when they were originally constructed.

Generally speaking I have avoided illustrating the more palatial buildings as examples of contemporary craftsmanship, because their very extravagance often makes them essentially un-English in design, and also because there are numerous excellent works adequately illustrating these vast interiors by photographs. I have, however, illustrated a few of the smaller rooms, possibly boudoirs or studies or little withdrawing rooms, that are still to be found in the larger houses because the are such perfect examples of the contemporary theme in miniature; they are the sort of rooms which might have been found in dozens of the smaller houses of taste and fashion as well as the mansions and palaces.

I should like to stress the point that this book is meant as a guide only for the student of domestic history. The illustrations, all taken from existing houses, are intended to give the form of decoration in use at certain periods so that the prevailing fashion can be more easily assimilated. It is my sincere hope that the reader will find sufficient information to give pleasure and interest to a further pursuit of the subject.

I

EARLY TUDOR 1485–1558

Although the fifteenth century saw the dawn of a new civilization in England, it was not until the succession of the Tudors that the rigid atmosphere of old Feudal England was at last dispelled.

The invention of gunpowder had almost at once rendered the previously impregnable fortress a useless barrier, and a diplomatic tolerance of one's neighbour's peculiarities replaced the earlier aggressive attitude of interference adopted by the young Knight of an earlier generation. The lengthy struggles between the Lancastrians and Yorkists had ended with the establishment of a strong centralized monarchy and at the same time served to drain the nobles of much of their accumulated wealth. Their lands were split up or confiscated to make room for a new class of yeoman farmers. Such noble families that had escaped this confiscation found their coffers so depleted by lengthy wars that they were no longer able to support their vast estates, and the land was divided and sold or let to anyone willing to take on the responsibility involved. Domestic security and the acquisition of those things that really contribute towards the physical comfort of the householder began to rank higher in a man's estimation than the possession of a fortified castle or a suit of armour.

It is therefore at the beginning of the sixteenth century that a new domestic enthusiasm is first discernible, no longer ruled by feudal lords and guided by religious teaching to the exclusion of every other form of education—but a new vitally competitive and constructional generation of freed men desiring to build themselves homes and establish families to work their lands for their own benefit and comfort.

Education began to spread even into the smaller towns and villages, aided to a considerable extent by the use of the printing press. The New World was discovered, and the idea of further discoveries and adventures on the high seas added zest to a life that had previously been governed by local interest only.

The vast halls of earlier times which had housed a hundred or more were no longer necessary. The house resolved itself into a less spacious but more intimate accommodation for the family and all those paid servants necessary to the upkeep of the household and farm lands. The draughty hall with its tapestry hangings and stone floors gave place to a more moderate-sized living room, panelled against the draughts, sometimes floored with oak or other local woods. Fireplaces with chimneys were no longer a new invention but a necessity that had to be incorporated in every new building and were often the centre round which the whole house revolved. The use of glass in windows, instead of horn and wicker, immediately lightened the atmosphere inside the house and emphasised the new furnishings so skilfully worked by the craftsmen of the time.

Although fitted furniture is considered a new idea in the equipment of modern houses and flats, this is very far from the truth. As early as the fifteenth century fixed settles or window seats were incorporated in the building of a house, as were cupboards both small and large—the salt cupboard beside the kitchen fire was a necessity when salt was of the utmost value and houses were not supplied with damp-courses to keep walls dry and warm.

In the Preface of Mary Evelyn's 'Mundus Muliebris'—a delicious commentary on the modes and manners of her time—John Evelyn, her father, has written in defence of the 'good old days' (obviously early Tudor) the following comfortable vision of his ancestors' domestic simplicity—'They (our forefathers) had cupboards of ancient useful plate, whole chests of damask for the table, and stores of fine Golland sheets "white as the driven snow" and fragrant of rose and lavender for the bed; and the sturdy oaken bedstead, and furniture of the house, lasted one whole century; the shovel-board and other long tables, both in hall and parlour, were as fixed as the freehold; nothing was moveable save joynt-stools, the black-jacks, silver tankards and bowls; and though many things fell out between the cup and the lip, when happy (?nappy) ale, March beer, metheglin, malmesey, and old sherry got the ascendant among the blew-coats and badges they sung Old Symon and Cheviot Chase, and danc'd Brave Arthur, and were able to draw a bow that made the proud Monsieur tremble at the whizze of the grey-goose-feather. 'Twas then ancient hospitality was kept up in town and country, by which the tenants were enabled to pay their landlords at punctual day; the poor were relieved bountifully, and charity was as warm as the kitchen, where the fire was perpetual.'

The sixteenth century witnessed perhaps the greatest change in our social history before the Industrial Revolution, and in the interval England produced a succession of craftsmen who, sometimes inspired by foreign example, progressed from style to style with a competent and beautiful technique leaving to the succeeding generation a high standard of skilled workmanship.

The new generation was athirst for information—the young apprentice eager to learn all he could so that he might become a master in a world that promised so much scope to the individual. Even the wealthiest families did not desire their sons to idle at home; everyone was expected to make his way in this newly found world of freedom. Frequently the younger sons of squires and merchants were apprenticed to some trade or craft so that in a very few years they were able to start on a career of their own. The Englishman's love of the countryside has always been instinctive and, whatever his profession, he has ultimately desired to settle in the country. It was this desire that led to the establishment of so many beautiful country houses scattered all over England. Each man as he made his way in trade or profession sought to end his days and spend his accumulated wealth in a home of his own where his eldest son might live after him and establish his family in suitable surroundings.

There is no period in architecture when this country followed its local individual themes with such entirely satisfactory results as that of the early Tudors. The charming grace of the timbered house still makes its very definite appeal, whilst the brick and stone houses with their mullioned windows and leaded panes have withstood the hand of time more effectively than the more ornate Italianate styles of a later date. Rarely was the small house devoid of character, for every man was something of a craftsman, though he could probably neither read nor write. Travelling craftsmen toured the countryside adorning the insides as well as the outsides of newly built homes, or those which were being brought 'up to date.' Hence we find mural decorations, pargetting and plaster-work obviously by the same hand in districts some considerable distance from each other, as well as the more obvious district covered in a comfortable radius from a town or city.

As the printed book became more popular wood-cuts and engravings which showed both architectural and classic detail helped those craftsmen in the more remote parts of the country to follow the prevalent styles, inasmuch as they were adaptable to the local stone and wood. We therefore find similar general designs used throughout the countryside at approximately the same date.

The merchant and the yeoman farmer with money to spare had their rooms made as comfortable as possible, and vast sums were sometimes expended on the fine furnishings of beds. These were hung with curtains to keep out any stray draughts and canopied above to protect the sleeper from the dust that might fall from the exposed rafters. Furnishings were still, in comparison with our present ideas, very sparse, and the acquisition of a fine four-poster bed was an event of some importance.

The chest, table, settle, joynt-stools and bench were the main furnishings of the living room, and any or all of these might be decorated with linenfold panelling and romayne work.

Towards the middle of the century where benches and stools had been used, the chair, at once more comfortable and personal, became a more usual feature. The long trestle table was more or less ousted by the framed table. In lesser homes wooden bowls and spoons for eating began to be discarded in favour of the pewter dish and spoon of silver or base-metal.

On a grander scale Henry VIII's example of employing craftsmen from other countries in his building of Nonsuch Palace, introduced an enthusiasm for the ornate. Foreign craftsmen often found a better and more comfortable living in this country than in their own, though we know that many of the finer Italian artists refused all bribes to brave the perils of this uncivilized island.

It was this first influx of Italian, Flemish or German settlers with their books and tradition of design, that created the desire for decorating all possible available space, both inside and outside the house. At this date it is often impossible to separate the actual work executed in this country from that which was brought over in the extravagant enthusiasm for the strange and costly.

Whole rooms were often lined with panelling which had previously been made for a house the other side of the Channel, but we can also see copies of these 'foreign' designs carried out so accurately by the craftsmen over here that unless some actual record exists as to their origin we cannot say they were 'made in England'. From the point of view of English Interiors we are not concerned with these finer points, for the room was built to accommodate such panelling and its very use has made it 'English.'

The facing illustration shows a typical example of a living room in a moderately sized house probably built in the time of Henry VII.

This room is of particular interest both for its lovely timbered roof and for the fine example of studding on the far wall. Here we see the earliest type of panelling, which consisted of bevilled oak boards let into grooved uprights which formed a partition-wall or screen between rooms. Its purpose was not, as was later the case with panelling, to cover rough timber and plaster or a stone wall. Examples of similar 'panel and post' studding appear all over the country and there are probably a great many houses that have this type of wall beneath a later application of lath and plaster. Bedrooms were often separated in this manner. (One of these we found in our own home—under lath and plaster of a very early date—when trying to cut a doorway into the next room.)

In this illustrated example, the panelling is used as a hall screen, its purpose simply to keep the draught from the front door out of the living room. Such screens were in use both in cottage and in the larger house, the original version of the ornate and beautiful hall screens still to be found in many old Tudor mansions.

THE CHANTRY, COMBE RALEIGH

The timbered roof with its intriguing arrangement of crossbeaming is decorated with four very beautifully carved bosses, each design following the medieval forms reminiscent of illuminated manuscripts. Some of these bosses have recently been 'restored' but care has been taken to make the restorations follow faithfully their originals, so that it is almost impossible to see any difference.

Both the fine moulding on the beams and the bosses are decorated in their original colours, gold, black, and brick-red. It would seem that these beams have never been covered, probably because of the odd slope of the ceiling. Unfortunately in many houses the fashion for plastered ceilings, at a later period, has meant many fine timbered ceilings have been ruined or defaced by nails driven in to hold the lathes for plaster, and the larger beams are marked by the adze used to roughen them enough also to hold plaster. When in the course of time the plaster ceiling has fallen and the old beams once again exposed, their condition is usually deplorable.

The decoration of the living rooms quite naturally was originally governed by the necessities of life rather than by artistic whim; it is therefore necessary to view such decoration from a practical standpoint.

First and foremost come light and heat—therefore the windows and fireplace are of primary importance. The open fireplace with its wide chimney was obviously the main feature because large logs were being burned here and space must be allowed for their comfortable disposal. As family life normally collected round the fireplace, its decoration, however simple, would immediately have an audience.

The earliest fireplaces of this period were either constructed with a perfectly simple great oak beam supported by stone work either side, or a large slab of stone flush to the wall with the chimney stack outside. The stone aperture followed the traditional fashion for opening, being a Tudor or four-centred arch, carved to suit the householder.

The surviving examples of these early stone fireplaces carry simple designs —usually geometric in shape, carved along the top slab of stone in a series of squares. In the smaller rooms the principle was the same, and on the next page are two examples of the four-centred arch stone fireplace in its most simple form. The first drawing shows the only ornament to be the fleur-de-lys carved at the springing of the bevil. This old fireplace found in an upper room was exposed during the alterations of a home in Dorsetshire. Just beside it was a doorway of similar design which had at some time probably been the opening to a stairway.

19

The second drawing shows a later and more decorated arrangement of the same idea still based on the perfectly simple principle of cutting a decoration on the face of the stone with a minimum of ornament.

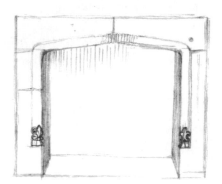

Simple Tudor Fireplaces

That there were fine carved oak chimney-pieces at this time is an undeniable fact, for one at least is still in existence and probably there are others. Failing, however, to find any others that might have adorned the smaller home I have included the 'Holbein' chimney-piece now at Reigate Priory—perhaps the most spectacular example of domestic carving which was carried out during the first half of the sixteenth century in this country. The story which originally led me to its 'discovery' was an entry in John Evelyn's Diary in 1655: 'I went to Reigate to visit Mrs. Cary at Lady Peterborough's in an ancient monastery well in repair but the park much defaced; the house is nobly furnished. The chimney-piece in the great chamber, carved in wood, was of Henry VIII and was taken from a house of his in Bletchingly.' This would probably refer to Anne of Cleves' home in Bletchingly, but the whole thing is so gigantic in scale and so exquisitely carried out in every detail that Nonsuch Palace with its wonderful collection of works of art would undoubtedly have been a more suitable background for such a masterpiece. In this magnificent example of early Tudor carving we can see to its full extent the Italian Renaissance 'adapted' for domestic use. All the ideas which were singly and together to become so fashionable in the next 100 years appear to be incorporated in this one example. The 'scrolled' design reminiscent of cut leather with edges rolled, which appears at the back of the seats and directly behind the shield was to become during the following century the main background for design.

20

Detail of Frieze
below Cornice

The 'Holbein'
Chimney Piece in
Carved Oak

REIGATE PRIORY   *c. 1540*

The 'strapwork' on the frieze is probably the earliest of its kind. Strapwork was the name given to the interlacing designs which were left in relief when the background was cut away in geometrical shapes. The charmingly childish decoration in plasterwork over the fireplace itself is essentially English—and a very early example of English plasterwork if not a copy of the original. Here we see the ability of the artist employed to represent, in detail, a clothed figure of the period complete with cap and feather, slashed trunk hose, and puffed slashed sleeves, but the nude figures are almost grotesque in their shapelessness. The twirls and fruits and figures sprouting foliage are typical of the conventional design at this time (about 1540).

Plasterwork on Holbein Fireplace   *c. 1540*

Plaster, of a sort, had been used in this country for centuries in such forms as wattle and daub, lath and plaster etc. It was composed of sand, lime and often hair to tie it together, dried hard but extremely brittle, and though it served its utilitarian purpose adequately it was not malleable to the hand. Its use as a means of decoration was not therefore immediately obvious, and it was not until Anthony Toto, a 'wax' modeller from Florence, was induced to come over to England to help with the decoration of Nonsuch Palace that the almost unlimited possibilities of decorative plaster-work were first realized.

The composition of the plaster used in Italy included powdered alabaster or white marble; as neither of these commodities were easily obtainable in England a mixture of rye dough and lime was found to hold much the same qualities the only remarkable difference being in colour (ivory rather than white) and the fact that it took much longer to dry.

Here then, ready to hand, was a new method of relief design, less arduous than carving and more effective on a grand scale.

As early as 1547 an English craftsman, Charles Williams was advertising his services to supply 'Internal decorations in the Italian fashion.' Such services were employed by Sir William Cavendish who referred to him as a 'Cunning Playsterer' in 1554–1556.

Windows were still heavily barred in the Early Tudor houses. Normally such bars were outside the glass and this can be clearly seen in the drawing below. Glass being comparatively new and expensive was only made in small sizes so that the small leaded pane, which might of course vary considerably in shape, was a necessary feature of all the windows of this period. Such glass was rarely pure white, a pale green or greenish yellow or some other pale tint was usual. Though thin and apparently fragile, these delicately tinted panes are still to be seen in many old houses. They must therefore have had a tenacity and strength considerably greater than some of the less flawed glass of a later date.

The ogee arches, at the top of this very beautiful window, are of course more typical of an earlier date than Henry VII but traditional styles in architecture died hard in the country districts and there probably were a great many windows with fine tracery stonework to be found at this period still being made for domestic purposes. The stonemason derived most of his knowledge from ecclesiastical architecture, and his early training normally consisted of making painstaking copies of existing designs which when once thoroughly understood lasted him a lifetime, and could be utilised again and again.

A much more usual design was that consisting of mullions and transoms crowned with a four-centred arch with cut-out spandrels. An example of this style appears at the bottom of the next page.

An interesting little window is shown at the top, with wooden mullions and iron bars inside, the glass cut in diamond and lozenge shapes, the smaller panes being originally all slightly darker in colour. A dropped shutter is encased in the wall below the window to pull up when required and hook onto the beam over the window. This is one of the earliest shutters included in the actual structure of the

Window at
BRADLEY MANOR, DEVON
Early Tudor

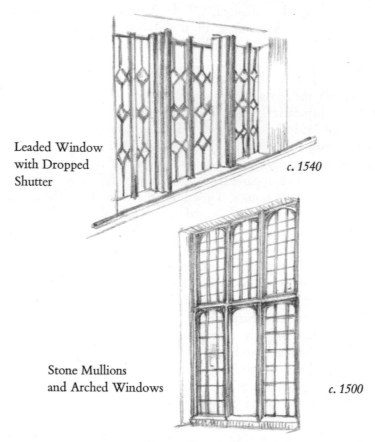

Leaded Window
with Dropped
Shutter

c. 1540

Stone Mullions
and Arched Windows

c. 1500

EARLY TUDOR WINDOWS

room though probably the hinged type were already in general use. As is so often the case where an example of early Tudor craftsmanship is discovered in a reasonable condition, it has been covered for centuries by a wall—this little window, with some of its original glass was 'discovered' in such a manner in a small home in Essex during reconstruction.

Linenfold panelling—which took its name and origin from folded material (possibly the folded napkin on the chalice),—soon lost its original form in the process of being copied. This can be clearly seen in the illustration where the same curves and shapes appear in the space beneath the carving but the 'linen' does not fold except in the gouged-out grooves. A variety of forms based on the original inspiration soon appeared and these have since generally become

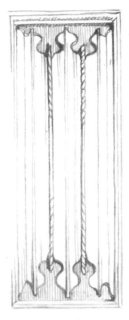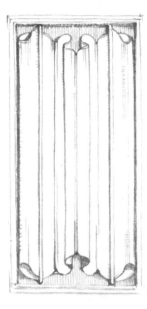

Mock Linenfold   Linenfold Panel

EARLY TUDOR

known as 'linenfold.' Other forms designed from rolled parchment and scrolls have much the same effect.

The design was achieved by cutting out the background leaving the edges as high as the surface and only cutting away a minimum of wood to leave the folds outstanding.

In many instances linenfold panels were used for covering the main surface of the walls and a more decorated line of panelling introduced as a sort of frieze or for the panels round the fireplace; sometimes a frieze at the top of the walls carried designs of heads after the Roman style. These were carved in roundels and called romayne work. Although their origin was Roman such heads show the contemporary form of head-dress then prevalent in this country often with a 'growing' or 'flowering' design so that spaces could be conveniently filled with an arabesque or leaf where realistic portraiture forbade.

This decorative style flowed into the majority of design and a pleasant and amusing fashion persisted, whereby a flower-head might prove on careful examination to be that of a jester in cap and bells, or a grotesque heavily maned animal, or a sleeping baby with bonnet frills. A dolphin could spout shoots, and a lady's coif burst into flower, for as long as spaces were filled with pleasant

25

A

B

C

Carved Oak Panels
and Romayne Plaque

EARLY TUDOR

shapes there was no need to accept nature as more than a guide to imagination. The mermaid and merman appear during the early Tudor period with increasing frequency, their curly tails making a fine starting off point for floral design and arabesque.

The growing fashion for heraldic design was also noticeable in panelling. Supporters of grotesque or human shape carry shields which might at some time have been painted but are now usually devoid of decoration.

All these features are found together in the magnificent oak screen at Bradley Manor in Devonshire which was probably started about 1530. The screen is comparatively small, being a partition between the old hall and its anti-chapel. Both sides are carved with similar designs, the chapel side not being quite so

BRADLEY MANOR
c. 1530

27

ornate. The lower panels are all imitation linenfold, the upper ones following the Italian fashion and being set between heavily carved uprights. The cornice at the top carries an essentially English design of oak-leaves and berries. The side shown here is in the hall just to the left of the great fireplace, its use definitely being domestic rather than ecclesiastical. Storks or herons, dolphins, cherubs, mermaids and shells, urns, bells, and a variety of flowers, fruit and foliage all bear significant witness of the Italian origin of the Early English Renaissance.

Another example of decorated panelling of this date is that which is now to be seen in the lounge of the White Harte at Uttoxeter in Staffordshire. Some of

Detail of Top Panel

EARLY 16TH CENTURY

28

Carved Door and
Details of Linenfold
Panels   *c. 1540*

this is obviously 'built-up' or faked but a considerable amount—including the door—is original. Stories as to its history vary considerably but the theory that it has been moved, possibly several times, from its original setting seems more than likely.

The carved heads on the doors reproduce the slightly grotesque head-dresses worn in the late 15th century in England and Northern Europe, and the top panels in every case show a design of tracery which bears out one story which claims that the panelling originally came from a church.

Similar panels of tracery do, however, exist in all types of Gothic domestic furniture.

The escutcheon and doorhandle both belong to a later date, but the cock's head hinge is a very fine example of polished ironwork of the period.

A simple and delightful little door of Early Tudor workmanship is to be seen preserved in Christchurch Mansion at Ipswich. This door is made up simply from six panels let into two uprights and a cross bar, a board at the top being slotted into the main structure.

The top centre panel is carved in the manner already described as Early English Renaissance; the five linenfold panels are all slightly different which suggests that the design was usually freehand and not copied.

The top board displays two supporters—a sort of cockatrice and some curly-tailed animal—holding an escutcheon and arranged in a semicircular cut out space. Cherubs heads with outstretched wings are carved in the corners. The original hinges are still on the door.

II

LATE TUDOR 1558–1603

As the sixteenth century progressed the desire for simple comfort became complicated by the introduction of the ornate and fantastic fashions from across the Channel.

Italy was acclaimed the leader of all artistic endeavour, but the classic ideal was neither comprehended nor properly interpreted by the architectural enthusiasts of Elizabethan England. Furniture and panelling and other household decorations became gradually more and more flamboyant.

The classic features that had inspired the Italian Renaissance could be seen half buried in intricate strapwork and copious clusters of fruits and flowers that now seem inseparable from the designs of the late sixteenth century, yet with all this the Elizabethan style as a whole remains obstinately English in spirit.

The East and West Indies with their promise of adventure and fabulous wealth lured many away from more rural pursuits, and silks and velvets, precious metals and other treasures, together with new ideas on architecture and hitherto unknown furnishings were finding their way into the homes of all those even remotely connected with the merchants of that time.

This was England's golden age, and if to our modern eye the interior designs and furnishings of the second half of the sixteenth century appear garish and over-decorated, we must remember that it was this very quality that made them of value to a still simple-minded people, in much the same way that a child is excited by a decorated Christmas tree rather than the straightforward fir or pine.

It is difficult at this stage to say exactly how much was truly English and how much was foreign in the furnishings and decorations of English homes. More often than not their furniture was a hotch-potch of pieces from various European cities with an occasional piece of solid English oak that served too useful a purpose to be ousted by ornate pieces from other countries.

Carpenters and journeymen and craftsmen everywhere were busy copying the new styles—a quaint Italian sideboard supported by caryatids or dolphins and made from walnut, a Dutch cupboard with gulled front, a French four-poster bed with curiously carved design in sweet chestnut and hung with finely embroidered hangings, a fine Chinese silk coverlet with golden birds and unbelievable flowers. The work they produced was magnificent, their interest and individuality imbuing the article on which they were working with a strength and vitality that has withstood the wear and tear of four centuries.

Inventories of furniture at this date give us the impression that the bedrooms and their equipment were still of more value to their owners than the furnishings of the living rooms. Much time and money was spent in the lavish equipment of the bed with its beautifully embroidered or tapestry hangings and coverlets.

The same colourful and complicated designs flowed in profusion on curtains and bedspreads. Frequently such designs were copies from some foreign book of ornament, but by far the most popular design included the native animals and flowers so dear to the hearts of every English countrywoman. These designs are particularly amusing in their disregard of proportionate values. Caterpillars as large as goats balance on apples half their length. Birds and squirrels perch on tiny flower-heads, bees, butterflies and a score of insects fill any possible gap that might occur between the trees and flowers. The flowers themselves include such everyday varieties as honeysuckle, cornflower, thistle, rose, vetch, iris and harebell, and we see the same arrangements of these popular flower shapes introduced into the plaster work of the time. Richly dressed little figures in wooden attitudes and unbending attire appear in all forms of contemporary design, from mural paintings to the embroidered seat of a chair or cushion, their ruffles and farthingales executed with a formal care that gives them an architectural quality.

Although panelling was generally so popular, tapestries were a speciality of both French and English design. Vast pictures were woven into these hangings, still frequently depicting scenes from the Bible or ancient mythology, with figures dressed in the farthingales and trunk hose of the day. The classic draperies for such figures did not appear in English design much before 1570, and even then not entirely to the exclusion of fashionable attire. The solid appearance of Elizabethan pageantry is a particularly interesting feature of these tapestries, which are in effect embroidered pictures with a decorative border or frame of equally busy design.

The dyes of this time were mostly somewhat dull and, though composed of clear elementary vegetable colours, were tinged with the grey or 'natural' tone of the wool before it was dyed. It was only in silks and linens that the clear clean colours were visible, and these are usually made more brilliant by silver and gilt threads, but a natural greyness prevailed in the tapestries which somehow enhanced their quality.

Mural Decoration
DOWLES MANOR *c. 1580*

Among the smaller Elizabethan houses the perfect gem, to my mind, is Dowles Manor in Worcestershire, with its delightful freehand mural decoration. Every room except the panelled living room has been decorated by the same hand, and though the rooms are small the decoration is in no way overpowering. Quite simply, the artist has set out to fill the space at his disposal with the contemporary designs of winged mermaids, urns, flowers, fruit and monsters. In one room a 'portrait'—possibly meant to represent the owner and his lady—appears and the figures are wearing the strangely padded garments so popular during the 1580's. Otherwise the designs hardly differ from those found in Ipswich—and might even have been carried out by the same hand.

There are comparatively few examples left in this country of Elizabethan mural decoration which have not been defaced or damaged by time or structural alteration. Many fragments have been preserved in museums up and down the country and several houses can boast of a wall or part of a wall which has at some time reappeared from beneath wallpaper or panelling, with its original decoration still in a reasonable state of preservation. But here at Dowles the decoration of the whole home has reappeared—from behind a complete inner

33

Typical Outline Mural Decoration
c. 1570

structure, built up apparently to cover the walls so that another mural decoration in the 17th century could 'modernise' the old-fashioned rooms.

As true mural painting has to be carried out on a newly plastered wall while still damp we must be grateful that in this instance the 17th century artist was either not prepared to obliterate the original artist's work or else he did not consider the rather uneven surface with its painted crossbeams a good enough background for his plastering. Whatever the reason the structure was, fortunately, not even discovered until comparatively recently when a new owner (an artist himself) was troubled by rats running between the two walls and on investigation the original paintings reappeared. The greatest of care has been exercised in the cleaning of the walls and now the designs are exposed once again in all their original clarity of colour; they seem actually to be part of the structure of the house, so well do they fit into the rough timbered walls. An interesting economy appears in the bedrooms; where the original four-poster beds must have been there is no decoration on the wall behind the bed-head nor did the artist attempt to pretend that there was. The design quite simply finishes in the space permitted in the same way that it finishes where an exposed upright beam is visible, although as the space is much narrower the design has to be altered in scale to fit. The whole scheme is so simple and intimate that it is absolutely right for this particular little house.

Harvington Hall, once an old manor house, within about 20 miles of Dowles Manor, would seem to have employed the services of the same mural decorator,

DOWLES MANOR, WORCESTERSHIRE

amongst many others. I have illustrated here one small section of a design that appears above a doorway: this is done in outline in black and blue, and although the mermaid has a more 'knowing' look than the charmingly vacant expressions on the faces of the 'owners' of Dowles, the design is very similar both in inspiration and execution.

Harvington Hall shows many traces of having, at one time, been decorated with mural paintings throughout—even the underside of a staircase. Another staircase shows the painted balustrades on the wall—an economy in oak balustrading to be found in many houses of the period. Here also are the traces of a series of beautiful outline paintings depicting the 'Nine Worthies.'

SUFFOLK
Late 16th Century

Mural Decoration, Black and Blue
HARVINGTON HALL *c. 1578*

I find these figures particularly enchanting, because they are (some of them) actually painted 'out of period'. The youthfully eager little soldiers behind a very juvenile 'David slaying Goliath' are wearing the long hose and helmets of the 15th century warriors and not the full padded garments of Elizabethan soldiery. They are beautifully drawn, what can be seen of them, with a firm clear outline, and the

35

Detail of
Chamfer

Typical Tudor Panels
BURFORD *c. 1560*

horses have the same sturdy grace to be found in the drawings illustrating the Winchester Bible.

From the comparatively simple and inexpensive fashion for mural painting we must now turn to the more sophisticated habit of panelling. Panelling having progressed from panel and post to linenfold and finely carved Italian styles,

CARVED PANELS
Late Tudor

37

settled down in early Elizabethan England to the squared panels sunk into a moulded frame with the lower edge 'chamfered' or sloped so as not to hold dust.

On the previous page details of the most usual type of panelling can be seen. The top panels were in most cases arranged to form a frieze and this frieze was ornamented in a variety of ways to suit the householder. Sometimes the upper panels were carved or carried incised quotations from the scriptures, sometimes they held very beautiful inlaid designs—bogoak, holly, boxwood and other contrasting woods being introduced into the design. Inlay at this period was frequently introduced into all kinds of furnishings, tiny pieces being cut out and placed into a recess already prepared; this type of decoration was an expensive business and required a really skilled craftsmen—it should not, however, be confused with the marquetry of a later date. Similar effects were often obtained by painting the upper panels. In higher rooms where the panelling did not reach to the ceiling we find that a frieze of plasterwork is frequently introduced; this might vary considerably in depth from a mere 6 inches to several feet.

As the century advanced the panelling of walls gradually became more complicated. First at regular intervals round each wall a pilaster was introduced; such pilasters in inspiration followed the Greek and Roman orders, Ionic and Corinthian capitals being the most popular. They in turn supported a cornice complete with frieze and dentils, but as the classic fashion continued to catch the fancy of builders and carpenters the original features were lost in a too enthusiastic use of other contemporary designs and motifs. Thus we find by about 1580 a pilaster covered with intricate strapwork design blossoming into a feathered capitol. The once simple squared panels were themselves carved and rearranged in a variety of shapes and sizes as can be seen in the accompanying sketches. One of the most popular shapes introduced into panels was that of the arch; this form was generally known as arcading and as can be clearly seen it again followed the classic example in principle, though far removed in design. Such arches sometimes contained paintings of saints, or brightly coloured urns of flowers, or a fragment of carving of the cut leather type.

The fashion for the decoration of panels did not, in the average home, exceed the popularity for a plain panelled wall with carved frieze and pilasters. The most frequently used frieze design was that either composed of pothooks interlacing, or a simply cut out long inverted U—this type of ornament in oak friezes is to be found in all parts of the country and the variety in design which so simple a motif can introduce is surprising.

Such rooms were still being introduced into new houses as late as Charles II's reign.

38

Detail of
Supporting
Capital

WHITESTAUNTON, SOMERSET
c. 1577

Often traces of floral designs are to be found on such panels—painted onto the plain oak in bright colours. Obviously at some time during the fashion for excessive ornament the owners sought to bring their plain rooms 'up to date,' without the expense of introducing new carved panels.

From the hundreds of wonderful examples of Elizabethan chimney-pieces still to be found all over England I have selected three,—one in carved Ham stone, another in plain oak, and one in Beer stone and plasterwork. I do not think any of these have been altered since their original installation. Each in its way is typical of the fashions and motifs in general use at that time yet they are all very different in style.

The fine stone example is the only remaining feature of a large room at White-staunton in Somerset, not a very large house though probably the manor at one time. All the accepted paraphernalia of the Renaissance is collected together with the entire equipment of the stonemason's books on design and heraldry, yet the whole is a magnificent piece of work and thoroughly English in its execution.

Conventional architectural details include Ionic columns, caryatid and atlante, dentils, egg and flower and leaf design. The fine heraldic display with supporters and full achievement of arms is of course the main feature of the design and the sheer weight of the stone bodies of the supporters makes this immediately obvious. The caryatid and atlante cut off at the waist, are supported by solid plinths decorated with twisted cornucopias brimming with flowers and fruits; this gives them a strength of design that otherwise might have proved a weakness in the general conception. They bear on their heads baskets again filled with fruit and flowers which in turn support the whole overhanging cornice. The underside of this cornice is decorated with equally spaced flower heads, each one different.

It is the base of this design that is really the background for the stonemason's skill; he has carved a wonderful frieze with infinite detail and a very proper appreciation for finish, such as the leaf at the curved end (shown in detail drawing) and the fine ridging of the ram's horn in the Ionic capital.

The interlacing pattern which appears behind the columns gives the added strength necessary for the support of the weight in the design above—without this the columns would appear too frail for their colossal job. The angry little bearded faces on the plinth below the foot of the columns again give a feeling of strength and vitality.

The whole ornate, and to our modern standards, overdecorated chimneypiece is typical of Elizabethan England.

The example in oak I found in a little farmhouse at Britford, near Salisbury in Wiltshire.

Built round an early tudor stone fireplace this example shows the same well balanced appreciation of design, though the scale and effect are both very different. The cornice here which fits into the ceiling is supported by eight little columns, Roman Doric in design, grouped in two's and standing on deep plinths.

Detail of
Strapwork

BRITFORD, WILTSHIRE
c. 1590

41

The frieze has a strapwork design which doesn't seem to repeat much but just flows in a series of geometric and looped shapes which might have occurred quite naturally as the carver removed pieces from the background, not adhering too closely to his traced design. The detail drawing here does not represent the actual design on the chimney-piece, but another of the same type finished with great skill. Books of such designs were easily obtainable and it was from these that the craftsman made his copies to suit his own limitations.

The strapwork design was Flemish or German in origin.

A more highly skilled piece of work is the very fine example in plasterwork taken from 'Grange' at Broadhembury in Devonshire. This gorgeous chimney-piece is now in a bedroom but it is believed that its original place was in the drawing room downstairs where a very fine example of 18th century design now stands (see p. 114).

The 'school' of plaster-workers or family who undertook so much fine plasterwork in Devonshire in the last 10 years of the 16th century and the first 25 years of the 17th, have collected their resources of inspiration and produced a decoration of great beauty in this particular example. Comparing this drawing with that of the stone chimney-piece at Whitestaunton we can immediately see the similarity in design although the medium in which it was worked makes a great difference to its actual construction and execution. There is a certain softness in the curves and lines of plaster work (often enhanced by a layer of dust) that prevents any one feature of the design from carrying too much importance. The design therefore flows rather than 'supports'. Here the Ionic capped pilasters are not intended to carry any weight but only to balance and contain the whole design.

The delightful little ladies—significant of Justice and Truth (Justice with scales and sword, and Truth with a mirror)—do not profess to support anything other than themselves though they stand as guardians to the highly decorative display of armorial bearings set out on a 'cut leather' or scrolled background and lavishly adorned with clusters of fruit and flowers.

Although figures appear quite frequently in the plasterwork of this period—this particular type of figure seems to be peculiar to Devonshire and neighbouring districts. They differ both in the very careful details of dress and in the arrangement of hair, which is waved high and in the Italian fashion of 1600. It is these—to me—striking dissimilarities to the traditional 'bundled' clothes of other plaster figures that give credence to a story that the Devonshire plasterworkers were an Italian family brought to Exeter by the Bishop to decorate his palace. We know that the Italian plasterworker was considered a very skilled artisan and that the English plasterworker was never very good at figure work.

Chimney Piece in Stone and Plaster
c. 1603
GRANGE, BROADHEMBURY

Plaster Figure, Devon

c. 1603

Carved Figure

Another example obviously worked by the same hand is this exquisite little plaster angel, one of a pair, that support the ceiling of a minstrel gallery at Widworthy Barton about ten miles from Broadhembury. She wears all the fashionable frills and furbelows, lace collar and cuffs and slashed French farthingale with ribbon ties, well padded shoulders, and a lace stomacher. Her toes are bare and hair 'undressed'. She is in every way similar to the Broad-hembury figures except that being worked in higher relief and also a shade larger (about 18 inches high) the details of her costume are more obvious. A curious feature of Italian fashions about 1600 was that when ladies all over Europe, and particularly in England, were busy piling their hair into a solid mass with no parting on top of their heads— which they could decorate with jewels and gew-gaws or a minute velvet hat—the Italian ladies parted and padded their hair to resemble horns—the centre parting with high springing 'waves' was so essentially Italian at this time that I feel sure the artist was an Italian.

The little carved wooden figure of approximately the same date (also with bare toes) shows how an English artist gets over the problem of an angel's hair 'do' by putting a crown on her head.

The plasterworker who carried out the amusing frieze in the library at Whitestaunton was obviously in no way concerned with the 'Devon' family (about whom I shall have more to say in the next chapter). His ideas again quite closely follow the florated Early English Renaissance designs, though with a skill and charm well in advance of the murals of that time. His animals—especially the fox and stoat are quite delightfully realistic, and though the camel is a trifle odd it is recognisable. The dragon or bird head sprouting flowers is often to

Detail of Plaster Frieze
WHITESTAUNTON, SOMERSET   *c. 1577*

be found in manuscripts as well as in mural decorations and lends itself very well to a design that has no other type of repeat as in this case; each division holds a different figure or group of animals but the dragon or bird head rises at regular intervals all round the room. This frieze is not more than 18 inches in depth and beneath it is plain squared oak panelling. The frieze gives light to a room that might otherwise have been a trifle too heavy.

45

Much has been written about the fantastic penduled plaster ceilings of Elizabethan England, but such ceilings were, normally, only to be found in the mansions and palaces, and not in the smaller house in Elizabethan times (though during James I's reign many of the smaller manors and even farmhouses and inns boasted at least one room with a finely decorated plaster ceiling).

When plasterwork was employed in the smaller house it was often used to cover and decorate the otherwise exposed beams on the ceilings and as a means of decoration in the square spaces that occurred between the timbers. Another attractive, though simple, fashion was to divide the ceiling by a series of ribs in low relief thus forming various shapes each holding a different design. In these, comparatively simple decoration casts were used to impress on the wet plaster a single design. Such motifs as fleur-de-lys, the Tudor Rose, or a simple flower design were extremely popular, and heraldic emblems and crests were frequently applied.

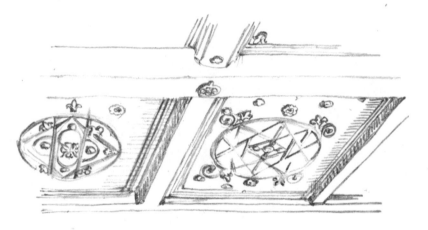

LATE TUDOR
(Fragment only)

The purely geometric design with tiny fleur-de-lys and Tudor Roses shown in the illustration opposite, repeats these two motifs only in very low relief, the plaster covering to the beams follows the line of the original moulding in the wood underneath. This example, taken from an old house in Worcestershire, shows clearly how the early plasterworker used his skill to decorate the existing features of a ceiling with two large casts and two or three smaller ones.

Of the panelled door of this time there is considerable variety, but many of these are no longer in their original position. The main features about the

PANELLED DOOR
c. 1580

Elizabethan door made it 'old-fashioned' within half-a-century—such features were its narrowness and lack of height.

Presumably the men of the 16th century were either all very short or else they habitually bent their heads to go through doorways, for there are very few Elizabethan doors still existing in the smaller home that the average man of today could walk through comfortably. Many of those I have measured are barely 5 ft. 6 inches in height.

Their simple construction of thin oak panels and a narrow bevelled frame-work made them very light in weight, and they probably rattled unnecessarily. They were however extremely attractive to look at. The illustrated example with its delicately carved top panel is not in its original setting; it was 'picked up'

47

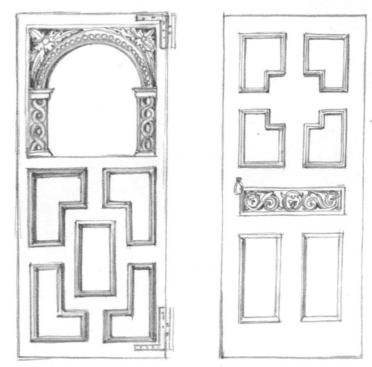

PANELLED DOORS
c. 1600

and now graces a bedroom at Dowles. The carved panel of flower and leaf design is in every way typical of Elizabethan country design, the same type of ornament might have appeared equally well in embroidery or plasterwork.

The more complicated panelled doors in this illustration emphasize the all-prevailing styles in Classic detail. The first example shows a decorated arcade its spandrels filled with a leaf design. The bottom panels are framed with a roundly moulded edge which stands up, rather as applied picture railing might do.

The second example is simpler and carries a strip of carved panelling in the centre—the ornament on this panel is based on the foliated scroll design which appears in both Greek and Roman architecture. The top panels have the same rounded moulding but the two bottom ones are sunk with a simple bevelled edge.

48

III

EARLY STUART 1603–1660

The beginning of the Stuart dynasty made no very remarkable difference to the modes and manners which had aleady reached a ripe maturity during Elizabeth's lengthy reign. Decoration was the same only 'more so.' That which we now call Jacobean was all an over-decoration of what had gone before—no lily was left ungilded, no beauty unadorned.

Taken singly each design, used in interior decoration, was often a masterpiece in itself, but where we find existing examples of rooms of this period with decorated ceilings and panelling as well as gigantic and heavily ornamented fireplaces, the whole is overwhelming and altogether too 'busy'. The simpler rooms that concentrated their decoration on either plaster ceiling and chimney-piece or carved chimney-piece alone are the most delightful examples of the period.

The desire to decorate everything continued fairly generally for at least the first twenty-five years of the century. Where examples of wall paintings occur these carry out the same or similar patterns as those seen already on the panelled walls. The colouring has lost the decisive tones of the Elizabethan murals and an almost sickly green and coral pink appear to predominate in the arches and spandrels, though some of the 'vase and flower' pieces are unexpectedly attractive.

In France tapestry was hung on walls almost to the exclusion of other forms of wall covering, but in this country both panelling and mural decoration continued in favour.

Sponsored by James I, tapestry workshops were opened at Mortlake by Sir Francis Crane to encourage the production of these still useful wall hangings.

It was also indirectly due to the King's interest in the arts that the traditional Elizabethan design with its lingering medieval influence was eventually discarded in favour of the new Palladian ideal as adapted to suit this country—a perfect lesson in proportion and ornament.

In order to appreciate the coming revolutionary changes (not of the Civil War but of design) we must hesitate here and look further afield.

49

As far back as the middle of the sixteenth century a new form of architecture had been well established in Italy. This was the classic revival as interpreted by Palladio(1515—1580) and since known as Palladian. Glimmerings of his example had—as we have seen in the previous chapter—arrived in this country with the classic ornament already described, but a full appreciation of his genius in domestic application had not yet been assimilated.

It was during the closing years of the sixteenth century that a young artist, by name Inigo Jones, was sent to Italy to study landscape painting; his interest and attention was immediately drawn towards the architectural wonders of Palladio, and on his return to England in 1604 he was employed by James I to paint and arrange the scenery for Ben Jonson's plays and masques, so popular in the English Court. His interests however still turned towards Italy, which he revisited in 1612. On his return to England he was employed as surveyor-general of the royal buildings. This position enabled him to lead English architecture by his example, and the ornament so dear to the builders and craftsmen of a few years earlier eventually gave place to the simpler proportions of a better interpreted classic formula.

Although Inigo Jones did actually carry out several of his own designs, there is a vast amount of both architectural and interior decoration which has been wrongly attributed to him. The comparatively few years between his return to England (when he was working on the Royal Palaces) and the commencement of the Civil Wars make it an impossibility for the artist himself to have been capable of so much work. What did happen, however, was the eventual adoption of the Palladian ideal in England because of Inigo Jones' research in Italy, but this was many years after his death.

Such revolutionary ideas could not easily or quickly be mastered, and it is possible that the intervention of the Civil Wars delayed their publication long enough before they were put into practice to render them more acceptable to the conservative mind of the average Englishman who, then as now, jibbed violently about accepting a fashion to which he was not already accustomed. By the time the Palladian was ultimately established, it had gained a maturity and grace on paper before actually being carried out. This might be the reason for the delightfully gracious buildings of the Restoration period that appear even now to be so neat and 'right.' Certainly the Double Cube room at Wilton which would seem to be Inigo Jones work (as it was finished before his death in 1652) has neither the simplicity nor the grace of a dozen less famous later examples based upon a similar set of principles.

The lesson to be learned from the drawings and examples of Inigo Jones' research, which apply to this subject of interior decoration, is one of Classic

HOARSTONE, STAFFORDSHIRE

Ornament introduced as domestic decoration in a comfortably proportioned setting. Previously the classic had been interpreted freely in the form of architectural features reduced to miniature to serve as decoration.

This particular period is one of the most difficult phases in our history to describe rightly, for there was the fundamental and tenacious hold of the Elizabethan ideas and ideals which had become so much a part of the people that any drastic change amounted almost to treason in the minds of a still superstitious and conservative country. Yet here we find the greatest architectural changes of a century about to be made. There are extremely few examples of this new type of architecture, only the very wealthty could afford to experiment and drive on with their purpose whilst the country was being torn apart by the Civil Wars, and such examples which survive today are all on the Grand Scale and not in any way applicable to this particular work.

At Hoarstone, in Staffordshire, a little farmhouse of charm and dignity boasts one upstairs room which still remains in all its original beauty. Another room downstairs has the same type of chimney-piece but it has been painted and has thereby lost its original clarity of design; also the panelling has gone.

The room upstairs, shown in the illustration, retains much of the tradition of the Elizabethan interior, in fact the only obvious differences by which it can be dated are the costumes worn by the Puritanical little figures introduced as caryatids in the design on the chimney-piece. These figures show unmistakable evidence that the chimney-piece was carved not earlier than 1630, possibly nearer 1640.

The whole room is panelled with small oblong panels set into a delicately moulded frame; the frieze is decorated with a small interlacing pot-hook design. The chimney-piece is obviously the main feature of the room and here the artist-carver has really let himself go, all his collected knowledge from the antique has been introduced skilfully with his feeling for traditional design and contemporary ornament. The whole is, however, essentially English. The three arcaded panels are intricately carved; the two side ones with be-flagged pediments supported on columns make a framework for flowers. The centre panel holds an urn of foliated growth. Each column supporting the egg and dart decorated arch is again carved with a leaf design and capped with Ionic capital. The four figures already described separate the panels. On the outside are two fauns, their arms upraised holding a small ornament, whilst the top is decorated with masks and looped dragons. These dragons appear in several of the houses in Worcestershire and Staffordshire and are considerably later in date than the majority of carved dragons elsewhere. This chimney-piece incorporates practically all the fashionable designs then in use, even to the strapwork panel

51

beside the fire opening, yet as a whole the pattern is so cleverly diffused by its quality of tone that it is neither too 'busy' nor confused .

Contrary to the general belief that all old oak tends to blacken with time, this little panelled room is still in its original state—a pale honey-grey tone. At no time in its history has it been spoiled by paint or varnish and the glow of three centuries of dusting has given to it a brightness in striking contrast with the majority of dark panelled rooms.

Many of the darker rooms that we find now in old houses were, unfortunately, in the last century treated to several coats of stain, in some instances to protect them from rot, but more often than not with the mistaken idea that oak should blacken with time and that artificial darkening was more 'romantic' than the rich warm grey of normally well-seasoned oak.

The furnishing of the early Stuart times were still mainly oak with, of course, such imported pieces as have been already described in the previous chapter. Decoration was lavish; the arcading and large bulbous legs and supports to such things as long tables, sideboards and four-poster beds were even more typical of this period than of the Elizabethan. Chairs were rather square and squat in shape—sometimes with upholstered seats; the first gate-leg table made its appearance about 1640. Carpets were rarely in use on the floor but were still much used as table coverings. Leather was used both for carpets and upholstery. Tapestries and damask wall coverings were hung in bedrooms and some of the smaller rooms, but panelling was by far the most popular type of wall-covering, even in the smaller house.

Although no cast was used to assist the workers who produced the two plaster overmantels illustrated opposite, their similarity is again too obvious to be overlooked. I have chosen these two examples out of several in the same Devon area to point the statement already made in the last chapter about this same family or school practising over a period not less than 30 years. These examples are dated 1591 and 1621 respectively. The earlier of the two is perhaps the happier, with its absurd little squirrels and the not too complicated scrolled design, certainly the ornament of Tudor roses, directly over the fireplace, is infinitely more suitable than the 'lace' design used in the Ham Barton one.

The latter has a very heavy background, more closely resembling ironwork, especially where the little 'studs' appear at the corners of the centre square. (Ironwork and armour were both very common in design during the Jacobean period). However, the design as a whole is perfectly balanced, the little faces on either side have the same flower-head quality that appear in the Early Tudor designs.

52

From Shute, Devon

PLASTERWORK   Ham Barton, Devon

Further north, but still in Devonshire, near Bideford, is another farmhouse with equally interesting plaster decoration. This is Southcott Barton which still retains three barrel vaulted rooms none of which is large. The most delightful of the three (some fifteen feet square) is decorated at both ends with a tudor rose design curling charmingly from a chimney-piece placed to one side of the wall. Although the larger room (not illustrated) has much in common with

53

SOUTHCOTT BARTON, BIDEFORD

the other Devonshire designs this illustrated example remains singularly
different.

Should the reader feel that I have concentrated too much on the Devon
plasterworkers, let me suggest that it is possible, even probable, that any thorough
local study would reward the student with a corresponding 'corner' in local
art in some specific form. That there were marked differences in the styles used
for plasterwork in different parts of the country at the same time is obvious
when we compare the four examples of plaster ceilings I have chosen here.

The Lounge of 'The Feathers' at Ludlow, now deservedly famous, must at
one time have been unremarkable when many similar examples were in existence.
The sectional divisions, covering the supporting timbers, carry a running
design of repeating scrolls and flowers, the pattern divisions are decorated with
the then popular vine and leaf which was not in the least unusual. What is most
striking to us today is the vast amount of design carried out between these
sections, the time and thought that must have gone to its eventual completion.
The plaster-worker seems to have been so in love with his work that he was

54

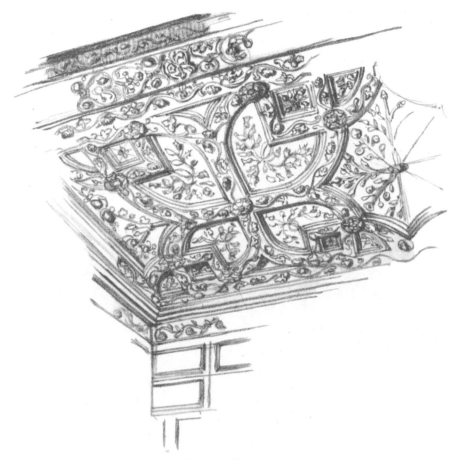

Plaster Ceiling
THE FEATHERS, LUDLOW
Early 17th Century

unable to leave it alone and had to go on adding to his design until every available space was filled.

The penduled barrel-vaulted ceiling from an upper room at the little farm house of Ham Barton near Newton Abbott is neither so simple as that at Southcott Barton nor yet so complicated as that of the 'Feathers' at Ludlow. The room is not large—possibly 15 by 24 feet in length—but nevertheless the plasterers have found the space to carry out their art with all its complicated details. There is even the display of the arms of James I on the end wall.

55

Detail of Plaster Frieze

Barrel Ceiling in Plasterwork
HAM BARTON, DEVON
c. 1621

Another similar piece of work (note the pendule with its suspended acorn) is that from The Grange at Broadhembury: here the same wooden casts have been used for the flowing decoration and the detail of the design on the dividing ribs is exactly similar in the two examples. Both these rooms were once panelled, and although The Grange is a much larger and more important house than

56

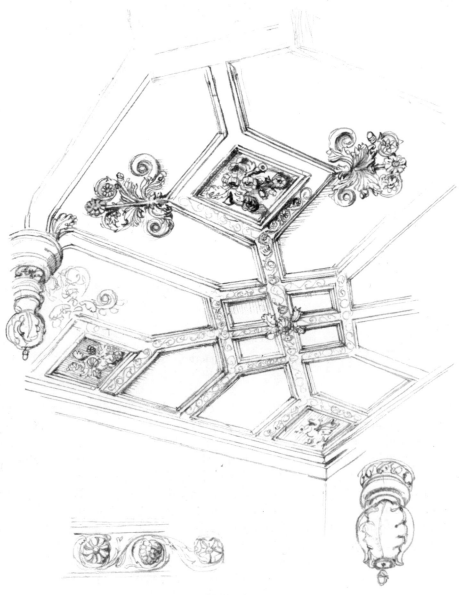

Detail of Design on Dividing Ribs

Plaster Ceiling
THE GRANGE, BROADHEMBURY
c. 1610

Plaster Ceiling
KING'S LANGLEY, HERTFORDSHIRE
c. 1610

Ham Barton could ever have been, it is extremely interesting to observe that the same plasterworkers were free to ply their trade wherever it was appreciated and there was no 'copyright' on any design employed.

The fourth example is one from King's Langley, Hertfordshire. Bearing the heraldic symbols of James I, the ceiling is divided into squares with a running pattern of flowers and grapes, on a slightly raised rib. The symbols are applied from a cast and are in low relief and although it is undoubtedly the work of Jacobean craftsmen it is still Elizabethan in conception, and delightfully simple in execution.

Comparatively few rooms decorated with the arcaded panelling of the early 17th century remain today in their original state. Many such rooms had their panelling removed within the century when the fashion for long panels commenced. We find fragments of arcaded panelling which must have been hidden for a couple of centuries, cropping up as overmantels and chests, bed-heads and tail boards, all re-constituted during the 19th century to make furniture suitable for the Gothic Revival. Many of those homes that retained their Jacobean panelling intact for three centuries, succumbed during the early years of this

58

The White Drawing Room
CHASTLETON HOUSE

century to the ever increasing demands (and prices paid) for the antique in America, and whole rooms were transported across the Atlantic to grace some wealthy connoisseur's mansion in the United States.

It was probably a style so ornate that few except the generation for whom it was originally installed appreciated its florid detail, but there were nevertheless a number of rooms of charm and character in spite of their concentrated decoration. One such room is that of the little White Drawing Room at Chastleton.

As far as is known this room has always been painted white, a rare exception to the universal use of seasoned oak at this period. There is a plaster frieze above

59

the panelling, and the walls of the room are divided by a carved frieze which is the same or similar in design to that on the plaster. The lower panels are plain all the way round including those on the doors. The ceiling is plain and the general effect is one of richness without being too ornate. Possibly if the room were larger it would not be so pleasing.

There were instances where, not content with the carved decoration alone, flower pieces were painted inside each arcaded panel and quite often the arcading was used as a frame for texts or paintings of saints. To illustrate this I have included a drawing from one of the larger rooms at Chastleton where every possible space has received individual attention either from painting or carving. The frieze contains a series of square pictures divided by carved caryatids and pilasters. All the centre panels have carved designs inside the central arcading. Groups of flowers appear in the surrounding panels—the whole is overpoweringly ornate. Although Chastleton House is undoubtedly a mansion, there were smaller country houses that boasted the same or similar decorations at one time in their history, but as I have already explained, there are very few examples left in this country that retain all their original features.

The window of Elizabethan England differed only slightly from that of the Early Tudor, but the Tudor arch and decorated spandrels had gone. Stone and wooden mullions were both used and small leaded panes in various shapes gave interest to the smaller casement windows. Larger windows throughout the country were mullioned with a transom or cross bar, occasionally coloured glass with the family arms appeared in the hall, but in the normal way the glass used was that same delicately tinted thin glass already mentioned.

This window with its finely moulded mullions and transoms is typical not only of Elizabethan time but of the Early Stuart as well, and although the sash window was said to have been first used in England during James I's reign it was not generally in use until the end of the 17th century.

The sash window was known in France at this time and often appears in the background of Abraham Bosse's famous engravings of the 1620—1640 period.

The panelled screen at Widworthy Barton was introduced into this house somewhere between 1600 and 1610 when the whole place was done up after a recent fire; by such events only can we definitely date these things. The design might easily have been that of 30 years earlier, or indeed 30 years later, as it is much the same as the Hoarstone room shown in the colour plate.

Obviously there were, at this time, many who preferred the old-fashioned oblong panelling to the more complicated shapes with richly moulded frame. In this particular room, the Hall, the ceiling was at one time plastered by the Exeter plasterers; members of the family who owned it some quarter of a century

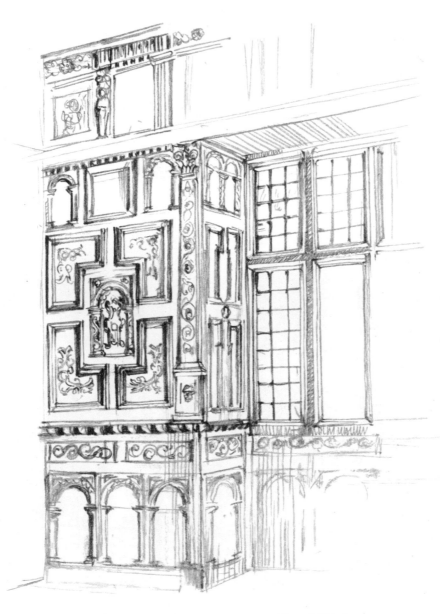

Carved Oak and Painted Designs. Stone Mullioned Windows

CHASTLETON HOUSE
c. 1603–1614

Oak Panels with Carved Frieze

WIDWORTHY BARTON, DEVON

ago remember when parts of it were still intact; now all that remains are the little plaster angels supporting the Minstrel Gallery, and a small section of plaster frieze on the inside wall of the gallery itself.

62

Early 17th Century

LOXLEY HALL, STAFFORDSHIRE

Of the design along the frieze at the top of the panelling, each section differs slightly and each section covers the space above two panels. The carving has unfortunately suffered rather from an overdose of dark stain and in some places the design is none too clear. Another panelled room in the same house is a

63

'made-up' room with at least three different types of panelling, all varying so slightly as to be unnoticeable at first. One wall has pilasters every four panels and the frieze looks as if it might have had writing carved on it once, which has been obliterated by centuries of paint.

It was most unfortunate that so many old houses were treated, in the last century, to a process of 'staining and graining' because when this was done the paint used had to be applied so thickly that any delicate carving was inevitably ruined, and it is practically impossible to remove without damaging the surface underneath.

Another case of 'staining and graining' was carried out at Loxley Hall in Staffordshire, and that which was once a very fine example of decorated Jacobean panelling is now so hideous in colouring as to make one forget the intricate design and skilled precision of the craftsmen who must have worked for many years there over 300 years ago.

This house has suffered very much from the hands of 'renovators'. Cupboards of 18th century design now cover the original 'arcaded' recesses, and though there is much of the fine 18th century style of interior decoration, the hall itself which should have remained a fine example of Jacobean craft retains only its intricate panelling and a made-up fireplace—all painted and grained in a particularly vile gamboge with shields picked out in brilliant colours, rather like a collection of postage stamps arranged round the frieze. From what one can see now (by opening the cupboard doors with their arcaded backs and carved pilasters and ornament) the hall must at one time have been very fine indeed though probably to the 'modern' taste that accepted the simpler styles at the end of the century it would have appeared over-decorated and démodé.

IV

LATE STUART 1660—1714

With the Restoration a considerable number of landowners returned to England from the continent to take up their residence once again and repair the damage that had been done to their confiscated estates during the years of their exile.

These years of exile in France and Holland had served—however unwittingly —to educate the Englishman to an appreciation of the French Renaissance as it flourished under the patronage of Louis XIV. This was a fine example from which to rebuild and decorate, as was the example of Italian building already set, though not so far appreciated, by the work of Inigo Jones.

The Plague as well as the Great Fire of London played their part in the clearance and dispersion of the old familiar way of life. The Plague was the cause of a number of fine new houses being built—away from contamination—in the home counties, and the Fire destroyed so many old homes that new ones had to be built in their place. It was a golden opportunity for the young and enterprising architect and artist, and, History repeating itself as it had done during the Renaissance in Italy, a host of men of artistic genius, many-sided in their comprehensive abilities, sprang into the limelight of fame. Of these Sir Christopher Wren (1632—1723), John Webb (1611—1674)—the talented pupil and assistant of Inigo Jones—and Grinling Gibbons had the greatest influence and effect on the architecture and decoration of the homes with which we are chiefly concerned.

Thus was the stage set, and within a very few years of the Restoration the old-fashioned house was an object of derision rather than an interesting antique. Apart from the fine examples of many existing houses of this time, we are also fortunate in the collection of records written by the rapidly growing educated classes. Much valuable information is to be found in the diaries of John Evelyn, Samuel Pepys, the 'Journeys of Celia Fiennes' and the many works of Daniel Defoe as well as a score of lesser known writers of this particular period. Each in their way saw the innovations of their time and recorded them with a wealth of intimate detail and very human criticism.

65

Carved Decoration
c. 1700

John Evelyn, indeed, did more than this, for it was due to him that Grinling Gibbons was 'discovered' working alone in a thatched house near Sayes Court, Evelyn's home, in 1671 and his work brought to the notice of both Charles II and Christopher Wren.

Grinling Gibbons, the most famous wood carver of this time, carried out most of his lovely carved decorations in lime wood.

The new scheme of decoration was one that concentrated on the ornaments around doors, windows, fireplaces, and pictures, also on a fine plaster ceiling with coved edge where a frieze had been previously.

Typical Panelling of Late 17th Century
BURFORD, OXFORDSHIRE

Painted ceilings were also to be found everywhere, but unfortunately few of these remain today except in the palaces and famous country seats.

67

Bolection moulding—a scrolled or curved fairly deep frame—surrounded each panel and such panels were now very large, no longer made of oak but other, less scarce woods, such as pine, cedar, walnut, chestnut, lime, etc. This new fashion was, in part, due to the scarcity of oak which had served its turn in the past to such a great extent. The country was going through a period of oak starvation. Too many trees had been felled for shipbuilding, house building, furniture and panelling, and not only this but vast quantities of oak had been absorbed by the iron-smelting works during the Civil Wars and little or nothing had been done to replant the woodlands laid bare during the political disturbance that had led to so many estates changing hands. Consequently we find that, although oak was still used wherever it was possible, new woods were being imported, and craftsmen and cabinet-makers were forced to experiment in various other types of wood which had not previously been considered suitable. The result on the whole was extremely happy, though fruit woods and pine have not the lasting quality of oak.

The idea of painting and varnishing woodwork was introduced with the intention of covering a grain that was not as fine as oak. Whole rooms were decorated to resemble marble, and this fashion was not confined to the larger homes alone. One of the most charming examples of this that I have found is at Nether Lypiatt in Gloucestershire—the sunk panels with their bolection moulding are the perfect groundwork for marbling. So skilfully has this been done that it is difficult to believe it is not actually marble. Later, in the 18th century, wallpapers were produced in quantity with much the same effects, though of course without the lasting quality of painted wood.

Another innovation for covering the irregularities of panelled walls was that of 'japanning' or lacquering; this became increasingly popular towards the end of the 17th century.

Floors were also a particular feature in these new homes, tiles or marble slabs were used in many of the downstairs rooms, particularly in the entrance hall, and fine inlaid floors of wood were arranged to display the family crest or some other decorative central design.

Niches and cupboards, book-cases, side-tables, and seats could all be built into these new rooms; there was, indeed, a considerable amount of built-in furniture—again this idea had been taken from the Italian villas. Niches were for the safer accommodation of 'busts' or objets d'art, for a new enthusiasm for such things had taken the country by storm.

Though silver and gold plate had disappeared from the dining table, it now reappeared in the elegant chocolate-pot, the tea service and the comfit-box or sweet-meat dish which held dainty sugared morsels to eat with the fashionable drink. Chinese tea services of fine porcelain were imported at great cost and adorned the table when the hostess was entertaining, but for the most part these priceless acquisitions were put away in a glass-fronted cupboard. This same cupboard was built to hold the more valuable table appointments and permit their beauty to be seen by all without danger to their fragile substance. This idea of alcoves and cupboards with shelves built into the rooms was fairly general from a few years before the close of the seventeenth century right through the eighteenth. Such alcoves quickly assumed an importance almost equal to that of doorways, windows and chimney-pieces and became a natural feature of the modishly panelled room.

Of furnishing, generally, we find three distinct phases. That of Charles II and James II, William and Mary, and Anne. The first was inspired by French example and a curled and scrolled decoration particularly suited to the curled periwigs and laced and ribboned ornaments of contemporary dress is marked. The second was frankly Dutch, and Holland had already been influenced by Orientalism, therefore we get lacquer and other Chinoisine interests as well as marquetry and parquetry and a considerable amount of heavier furniture as well. The third phase, that of Queen Anne, is the walnut era, brought about after some years of experiment in many types of wood, because of its very lovely grain and variety in colour. The furniture now termed, rightly or wrongly, Queen Anne, is of incomparable elegance and charm. The cabriole leg with its claw-and-ball foot was of Chinese inspiration, but quickly became Anglicised when reduced to a minimum of ornament, and the scallop-shell, that much used motif, appeared on the 'knee'.

There are a considerable number of mirrors from the time of Charles II still in existence, and many of them were decorated with amusing portraits of the King and Queen executed in stump work and a fine embroidered framework finished with some elegant wood or tortoiseshell. Embroidered pictures of the same type were a special feature of the smaller or more intimate rooms.

Pepys had his panels decorated by the contemporary landscape artist, Henry Dancre, who painted pictures of the Royal Palaces to fill the framework of four panels. These pictures were carried out in a sort of tempera medium, for Pepys mentions that although he preferred the appearance of an 'oyle' picture, 'Dankers' was going to paint these particular pictures in distemper mixed with egg 'to keep off the glaring of the light.'

An extract from Pepys' Diary on January 22nd 1668 gives us a pretty insight into the added pleasure of an elegantly appointed room and table. 'To the Exchange, calling at several places on occasions relating to my feast tomorrow, on which my mind is now set; as how to get a new looking-glass for my dining room, and some pewter, and good wine, against to-morrow; and so home, where I had the looking glass set up, cost me £6.7s.6d. At the Change I met with Mr. Dankers, with whom I was on Wednesday; and he took measure of my panels in my dining-room, in the four, I intend to have the four houses of the King, White Hall, Hampton Court, Greenwich and Windsor. Mightily pleased with the fellow that came to lay the cloth, and fold the napkins, which I like so well as that I am resolved to give him 40 s. to teach my wife to do it.'

During the Stuart period, the refinements of table appointments and kitchen ware had assumed a new importance. Elegance was the fashion rather than ostentatious display, and such items as glass and china were of the utmost value in the gentleman's house. The heavy glitter of gold and silver plate typical of the courts of Elizabeth and James I—and the wealthy merchants and squires of their time—had disappeared except for court functions. New requirements in table manners and habits had introduced the glass rather than the tankard and the spoon and fork rather than the fingers and knife—pewter was, however, still in use and continued in favour until the mid-eighteenth century.

English pottery or stone ware was being produced at the Staffordshire potteries before the Restoration, for we find in 1661 that an Act of Parliament was passed to prohibit the weight of stoneware butter-pots exceeding six pounds so that they might . . . 'contain at least fourteen pounds of butter.'

Fulham ware, both stone and salt-glazed ware, was produced by John Dwight as early as 1671, and half a dozen or more potteries were in production before the close of the century.

The majority of these early pieces were, however, fairly cumbersome and found their place amongst the larger dishes and such things as posset-pots and tygs (many-handled cups made for a hot drink).

Designs for embroideries to decorate chairs, beds and curtains took on new colours and shapes; many of such designs were copies from Eastern and Oriental imported goods; many were taken from the design books which were becoming more and more common. The large designs with flowers, birds and fruits of brilliant colours worked on white or neutral materials in wool—and now irritatingly referred to as 'Jacobean'—were commonly to be found in every home. The fine twill employed for bed curtains and appointments has lasted through the ensuing centuries with little harm, and where the embroideries were executed in silk and metal thread such works have defied the hand of time and the work of moths.

Generally speaking such designs followed the imagined shape of tropical flowers; pomegranates, pineapples, birds of paradise and the glamorous and brilliant denizens of other countries. Such shapes of necessity became formalised

70

Bradley Manor, Newton Abbot

because there was no actual fruit or flower available for the artist to copy, his or her ideas were inspired only by another's knowledge of such things helped by a colourful imagination. Hence we find purple or scarlet pomegranates with orange or green seed-pods, blue pineapples with magenta leaves and other improbable combinations of colour that add to the charm and general effect of the delightful designs.

Bradley Manor, Devonshire, boasts this unusual but very striking little square room with its hanging swags of plasterwork. Now called the Bridal Chamber it must have been introduced into the old Tudor house for the benefit of a bride in the time of James II or William and Mary.

The plasterwork is beautifully worked on a copper wire frame and it stands right away from the coved edge of the ceiling, adding much to its charm and character by the deep shadows cast from the flowers and leaves which are modelled in the round and not just in relief. In the four corners of the room are giant scallop shells slightly tilted forward to fit comfortably into the curve of the ceiling. The walls are panelled with large panels surrounded by bolection moulding, and their simple dignity balances the weight of plaster ornament to perfection. Probably the panelled walls were always painted—they are a dove-grey shade now—but it is of course possible that they were once uncovered.

Although the design is charming and the plaster-work a thing of beauty, there are comparatively few existing examples of this type of plaster-work. It was in all probability very tiresome to work or else got damaged too easily; that wire was often used in the smaller designs of the time in the early 18th century is obvious but I have not so far been able to find another example of this sort with such giant flowers carried out with so much detail.

A charter was granted in Charles II reign which forbade any person from practising as a plaster-worker unless he had served seven years apprenticeship. This prohibition very naturally encouraged a far higher standard in the work than might have been previously expected, though one finds that plaster ceilings tend to get more and more complicated in design as the century progresses.

A comparatively simple example based on the earlier styles and still incorporating the original covered beams in its design, is that of the ceiling in the old drawing-room at Sparrow House, Ipswich (now known as the Ancient House).

Here we have what might be considered a perfect 'transitional' example between the time of Charles I and the Restoration. The ornament on the plaster covered beams is the variation on the old theme of oak leaves, Tudor rose and thistle.

The centre of each division is decorated with an oval of rather clumsy looking fruit (this effect may be due to too many coats of whitewash in the past and not

Detail on Plaster

SPARROW HOUSE, IPSWICH
c. 1660

entirely the fault of the artist), and the four corners in each case are decorated with cartouches.

Now one of the famous examples of plaster ceilings of 1650—1660 is that of the Saloon at Coleshill in Berkshire, built by Sir Roger Pratt after consult-

Detail
of Corner

Plaster Ceiling
HINTLESHAM HALL, SUFFOLK
c. 1686

ation with Inigo Jones, and the oval wreath is there as well as the cartouches, so it would appear that the Sparrow House room had its ceiling put in about that period. The walls are panelled in the old style and the bow windows are particularly charming still with some of their old glass and original ornamental catches.

A much more sophisticated plaster ceiling—and this time happily dated beyond all question—is that in the drawing-room at Hintlesham Hall in Suffolk.

Designed for one Henry Timpersley—who was the then owner in 1685—his initials are introduced into the square in the corner. The ceiling edge is again

73

coved although decorated with different designs at the top and bottom of the curve. The coffered ceiling with its oval wreath of leaves, fruits and flowers is typical of the rich design of the time—possibly rather overpowering but balanced to a degree by the plain panelling of the walls below.

The fashion for great panels with bolection moulding was universal in the time of William and Mary and the only permitted originality in the general scheme of any room was in its 'ornament'—its fireplace, doors and windows in the simpler rooms, and the decorated surrounds for such features in the more splendid apartments as described by Celia Fiennes.

Her admiration for Chippenham Park gives us a fine picture of the 1690's—

'. . . the hall is very noble paved with freestone a squaire of black marble at each corner of the freestone; there are two fine white marble tables veined with blew, its wanscoated with Wallnutt tree the pannells and rims round with Mulbery tree that is a lemon coullour and the moldings beyond it round are of a sweete outlandish wood not much differing from Cedar but of a finer graine, the chaires are all the same; its hung with pictures att full proportion of the Royal family, all in their coronation robes from Charles the First to his Majesty with the Queen also, and at the end is Prince George and Princess Ann, in their robes of crimson velvet and Dukel coronet as Duke and Dutchess of Cumberland; the whole house is finely furnish'd with differing coulloured damask and velvets some figured and others plaine, at least 6 or 7 in all richly made up after a new mode; in the best drawing roome was a very rich hanging gold and silver and a little scarlet mostly tissue and brocade of gold and silver and border of green damaske round it; the window curtain the same green damaske and doore curtaines; there was no looking-glass but on the chimney-piece and just opposite in the place a looking glass used to be was 4 pannells of glass in length and 3 in breadth set together in the wanscoate; the same was in another drawing roome which was for my Lord; the dineing roome had this looking glass on the two peers between the three windows it was from the top to the bottom 2 pannells in breadth and 7 in length, so it shews one from top to toe; the roomes were all well wanscoated and hung and there was the finest carv'd wood in fruitages herbages gemms beasts fowles etc., very thinn

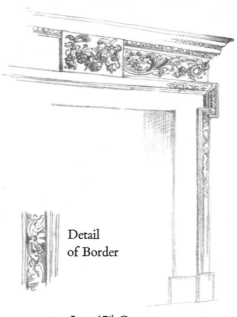

Detail
of Border

Late 17th Century
Fireplace

Carved Fireplace in Blue and White Marble

NETHER LYPIATT, GLOS

c. 1690

and fine all in white wood without paint or varnish, the severall sorts of things thus carv'd were exceeding naturall all round; the chimney-pieces and sconces stand on each side the chimneys and the glasses in those chambers where were loose looking glasses, which were with fine carved head and frames some of the naturall wood other gilt, but they were the largest looking-glasses I ever saw; there was a great flower pott gilt each side the chimney in the dineing roome for to sett trees in; the great curiosity of this wood carving about the doores chimneys and scomes together with the great looking glass pannells is much talked off and is the finest and most in quantety and numbers

75

thats to be seen any where; there is very fine China and silver things and irons and jarrs and perfume pots of silver; the common roomes are all new convenient and neate with double doores lined to prevent noises; the staircase is wanscoated, very noble fine pictures,...'

At Nether Lypiatt near Stroud in Gloucestershire is a perfect little house of this period. Built about 1690 it still holds all its original features unspoiled by time and kept perfect by a succession of careful owners. In the hall is a sculptured marble fireplace, the central decoration of a swag of flowers and scallop shell is carved in white marble set into a background of palest blue. The rest is white, and the whole gives an impression that might have inspired the original Wedgwood design. It is the only ornamental feature in a beautifully proportioned setting. The panelling is of pine and has been waxed for two and a half centuries so that its rich honey-colour glows with reflected light. The original brass locks and hinges are still on the heavy doors with their wide moulded frame.

Another room, the Library, holds at one end a pedimented bookcase, supported by simple pilasters, again a single feature of predominating interest and classic simplicity.

Many of the rooms are painted but those that have been waxed only are, somehow, more alive, for they catch and reflect every flicker of a flame, and glow when the sun shines.

Another well preserved house which must have been built more or less at the same time is Momperson House in the Close at Salisbury, Wiltshire. This house (now wisely chosen as the new Bishop's Palace) is much the same size as Nether Lypiatt but differs considerably in its scheme of decoration.

Doors and windows have skilfully carved frames, plasterwork has been used on ceilings and on the walls of the staircase. There is a carved overmantel in the

Detail of
Classic
Adaptation

76

drawing-room designed to frame a picture or portrait, and a sculptured classic design with head and basket of flowers and fruit in a front room. This had, when I saw it, been picked out in colour, which unfortunately did much to destroy its original rhythm, but the beauty of the design is remarkable in spite of the paint and shows the very great skill of the artist employed.

One of the really charming details in this particular house is that of the scallop-shell on the staircase. There is rarely a design of this time that does not include the scallop in some form or other but in this particular instance its design in triplicate is unusual and it reminds one more than ever of the ladies head-dresses of the time—upside-down the inspiration is too obvious to pass without remark.

The long sash window (illustrated overleaf), one of the most important features of the newly built house often claimed its share of classic ornament. In this instance the mouldings are all based on designs that appear in the architectural

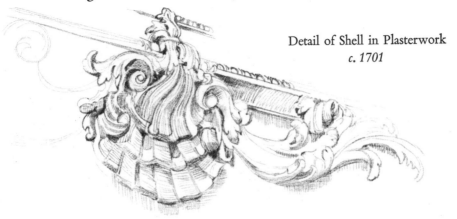

Detail of Shell in Plasterwork
c. 1701

MOMPERSON HOUSE, SALISBURY

ornament of Ancient Rome. The egg and dart, laurel leaf, and acanthus, but in each case they have slightly differing detail which gives them originality.

This little two-panel door with its rail between the panels is in a charming late 17th or very early 18th century house, Wadfield in Gloucestershire. The door is light, possibly made from pine or cedar and painted white as is the rest of the panelling. This is in all probability the work of a country cabinetmaker who was familiar with the new type of panel shapes but was not working with the fashionable type of thick wood. He therefore 'added' the moulding round the panels and two strips the length of the door on both sides which gives the door a certain thickness.

77

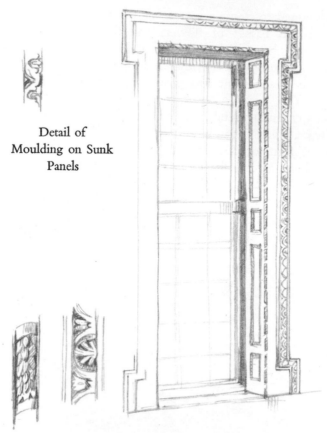

Detail of
Moulding on Sunk
Panels

BISHOP'S PALACE, SALISBURY

c. 1701

Doors, generally speaking, of the late Stuart period were much heavier than those of an earlier date. This in part was due to the new fashion in panelling which had a very much bolder and deeper moulding and therefore had to be carved from much thicker wood.

It was also due to the increasing use of imported hard-woods particularly mahogany, which, being much bigger trees, were brought to England in larger planks or sections than any of our indigenous trees. Mahogany, which is one of the heaviest woods in the world, was brought to England sometime between 1660—1670. Dr. Gibbons, the famous son of a famous organist, one of the earliest experimentalists in this new wood, had intended to use mahogany in the construction of his new house but owing to the extreme hardness of the wood

78

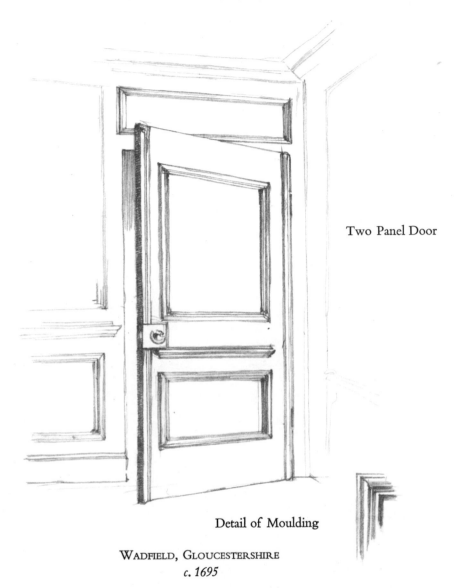

Two Panel Door

Detail of Moulding

WADFIELD, GLOUCESTERSHIRE
c. 1695

the workmen declined to use it. Its beauty of grain, however, was such that after the first tentative experiment (a candle-box for Dr. Gibbons carved by a cabinet-maker named Wollaston) it was quickly adopted by the finer craftsmen of the time and, later when its values were fully appreciated, was used particularly for veneer work.

79

Detail of
Door Frame

EIGHT PANEL DOOR
c. 1680

The beautifully designed door and doorway from a London house which is much the same date, has all the elegant proportions and fine carving typical of the Wren tradition. This door is heavy, the eight panels are sloped at the sides to fit into their moulded frames and yet leave the main surface of the panel flush with the main structure of the door. The design round the architrave—or moulded door frame—is particularly pleasant in proportion, and follows the formula for classic ornament in a leaf design.

The very heaviness of this door makes its setting of wide carved architrave a thing of balanced beauty. Had the door been of the flimsier type of the early Stuart period such a framework would have been utterly out of place.

80

V

EARLY GEORGIAN 1714—1760

The close association of fashionable English society with the culture of the continent had an outstanding effect on every form of art in the eighteenth century. Not least of this effect was architectural, and the various arts that were employed to alter the aspect of the home are too numerous to illustrate. Several styles or fashions in interior design do, however, predominate. The classic, natural outcome of the 'Grand Tour' which included visiting the wonders of Italy, was interpreted freely and individually and included the various types of decoration which appealed most forcibly to the individual concerned. Such personal appreciation might be concentrated on a fine columned room with marble floor and imitation marble walls with niches to hold a piece of sculpture rescued or filched from its original ruin. Or it might merely take the form of a collection of 'prints' taken from paintings of famous Italian landscape artists. It was to this audience of interested converts to Classicism that William Kent and his patron, the Earl of Burlington, published the works of Inigo Jones in 1727 and within a very short space of time the illustration appeared in reality carried out in detail in various houses throughout the country.

This period was, to a considerable extent, one of grandeur and wealth but though we are not concerning ourselves with the already famous Palladian mansions, the general effect and ideas are noticeable even in the smaller house due no doubt to published books and illustrations that could be used by local craftsmen as working drawings.

One of the peculiarities of the age was a potent desire for imitation; not only did such imitation include the obvious methods of following fashion but it was extended in all possible directions. Should a grand scheme of decoration appeal in style to the owner of a small house with limited funds, he did his best to carry out such a scheme with paper, paint and stucco or any other means at his disposal.

If he were unable to afford fine frames for pictures, or marble statues he had them painted on the wall.

Many of the smaller rooms were hung with silk or damask—or papered. Wallpaper was just beginning to come into use, for although patents had been taken out as early as Charles II's reign for the manufacture of wall-papers they were both expensive and probably tiresome to use, being printed in small squares about 12 to 16 inches in size. During the reign of Queen Anne a tax was levied on the manufacture of this new form of wall decoration at the rate of 1d. a yard and a few years later 1½ d.

When William Kent decorated Kensington Palace for George I the great Drawing-Room was papered, so obviously a wallpaper was not too insignificant to be considered a suitable decoration for a palace.

The earliest known wallpapers have been found decorating Tudor houses, but these fragments, interesting as they are, cannot be considered as a typical form of decoration at that early period, for paper itself was too scarce and difficult to manufacture to make it a reasonable commercial proposition. In fact the only paper made in England was brown paper. When the Huguenots fled to England after the Revocation of the Edict of Nantes in 1685 they brought with them the art of papermaking and the composition of such paper at that time was as interesting as the plaster used by the Italians 150 years earlier. Rags, oatmeal hemp and ground bread all pounded together and pressed between folds of woollen materials produced larger sheets of paper than had previously been seen in this country. The earliest designs of wall-paper were printed by wood blocks or stencilled, and if colour was introduced this was applied by hand. A great many papers were all hand painted but in their earliest form the general idea was to imitate fabric or copy some Chinese design. In order to make the illusion of fabric more realistic we find a very great percentage of wall-paper was 'flocked'.

Unfortunately for posterity a considerable amount of the fine carved ornament —which had been so much appreciated in the late Stuart interior design—was stripped away from the walls it had graced in the wave of enthusiasm provoked by the revivalists of Inigo Jones. The Palladian ideals would not countenance ornaments other than those which had originally been suitable to the classic formality of ancient Greece and Rome. (Even if such ornament were only paint or paper). We therefore find the nude and draped figure and the instruments and impedimenta of a civilization of two thousand years earlier applied as decoration to the homes and gardens of the eighteenth century.

This fashion for the pure classic, however, soon had its rival exponents experimenting with the 'rococo' styles, obviously more suited to the more intimate rooms where minute floral detail and leafy curls and scrolls could be enjoyed individually without detracting from the general magnificence of a large room or hall.

The skill with which these complicated designs, with but little cohesion, were carried out is considerable. Even examples in the remoter parts of the country leave one incredulous that there were so many skilled craftsmen ready and competent to copy a new formula of such profusion of detail within such a very short period of time from its original introduction. Not only woodwork but plasterwork and furniture and porcelain were all arranged to fit this type of rococo room.

It was into this atmosphere of country craftsmanship combined with classical formula and oriental splendour that Chippendale made his way, happily combining the three apparently violently opposed ideals into a whole that was at once delicately beautiful, original, and eminently suitable to our needs and climate.

Some of Chippendale's earlier works show the faults of a too hasty enthusiasm for the oriental as opposed to the capacity of the craftsman and materials to hand, but it is much a matter of personal like and dislike as to the superiority of his Chinese Chippendale style over those carried out so happily in an English vernacular, or *vice versa*.

Rightly speaking the majority of the work he inspired was carried out after 1750 when carpenters and craftsmen all over the country were doing their best to copy his style and drawings as published in his Directory in 1754.

Cedar, pine, cherry, walnut and other fruit woods were now used extensively for this lighter type of furniture, and no room was considered furnished without its tripod tables, fine winged armchairs and footstools. Whilst the wealthy displayed their knowledge and interest in travel by importing various curiosities and *objets d'art*, the average English householder decorated his home with the true English type of furniture that can still be found in many of our country homes, its fine craftsmanship having survived the ordeals of 200 years wear.

The Chinese influence was at its strongest in the middle of the century, the beauties of the Ming dynasty had been lauded to the skies with disastrous results for China had unfortunately become aware of the growing market from across the seas and they were briskly exporting anything and everything at fabulous prices for the hungry European market. The good was mingled with the bad with complete lack of discrimination, and copies were being made by practically every factory in Europe. But such manufacture was still confined to the smaller articles such as bowls and figures, tea services and dinner sets, or lacquered boxes to hold my lady's gloves and kerchiefs, patches and powder.

Few indeed were the homes where a Chinese fan or lantern could not be found or an elegant picture on rice paper or Japan silk, but probably fewer still were the homes that could really boast with truth and honesty that such refinements were the real thing and not a copy.

The fashion for Chinaware and porcelain was simultaneous with its production in Europe, for the first porcelain factory was established in Vienna as early as 1718. In England porcelain factories at Bow and Chelsea were active in the 1740's.

Defoe comments upon the fashion for china in his 'Tour of Great Britain' (1726) remarking that—'The Queen brought in the custom or humor, as I may call it, of furnishing houses with China ware which increased to a strange degree afterwards, piling their China upon the tops of cabinets, scurtores and every Chymney Piece to the top of the ceilings and even setting up shelves for their China ware where they wanted such places, till it became a grievance in the expense of it and even injurious to their Families and Estates.'

The curtains and soft furnishings and often wall coverings of this time were frequently prints. Indian prints were particularly popular, and so were the hand-printed linens, their designs taken from a Chinese pattern or copied from a contemporary pastoral picture. The pastoral influence was as strong as the Chinese, and we find the two themes running side by side for more than half a century. Elegant bunches of flowers tied by loveknots hang over the courting shepherd and shepherdess. Shepherds' crooks with bows of ribbon and jumping lambs wave over the heads of cupids or fauns. The lovesick traveller leans elegantly against the ruins of an Ionic temple, a rounded Venus or Cupid shoots arrows into a cornucopia which overflows, scattering flowers and fruits or musical instruments all over the woven surface of the printed material. Such prints were frequently carried out in one colour on a white or tinted background —the whole at a distance giving the impression, however misleading, of a Chinese design.

There were of course a great many people who still preferred the hand-embroidered materials for household decoration and particularly was this fashionable for chair seats, fire screens and footstalls, where rich baskets of fruit and lovely flower pieces vied with the splendours of the classical ornament or the more delicate rococo carvings and plaster-work of the smaller rooms.

About the year 1725 the lovely old house of Chillington, Staffordshire—home of the Giffard's since the twelfth century—was renovated in the latest style.

Amongst other modish alterations at least one room was papered with the latest thing in 'flocked' wallpaper, and this delightful room is still in a perfect state of preservation. Neither colour nor surface has suffered from the comings and goings of the centuries.

It is extremely fortunate that the same family has been in possession of this house ever since it was built, for it still retains records and dates of alterations and we can be unquestionably certain of their accuracy.

The room in the illustration is not large and the wallpaper arrangement is particularly interesting in that it was obviously originally included in the

CHILLINGTON, STAFFORDSHIRE

scheme of this actual room and not merely used to cover completely the walls, as was later the case. It fits into the spaces where the walls are not panelled between the doors and a panelled wainscot. In the small space between the windows where the wallpaper design would not be seen to advantage, panelling has been used. What actually happens is that the papered sections are 'framed'. A deep cornice runs right round the room and each door has a panel above so that no small space is papered.

The wallpaper is 'flocked' and gives an effect of cut velvet, the idea being to imitate material. Such papers were manufactured in considerable quantity a few years later for the French market and were called *Papier d'Angleterre*.

The process used for their manufacture was simple. The design was painted or stencilled in varnish, glue or some such tacky substance, then finely clipped wool was sprinkled onto this tacky surface and blown to remove the surplus 'flock'. In the early examples the flock surface was hand-painted after it had dried on to its background—in the later examples the flock was dyed before it was applied. In either case the effect obtained closely resembled velvet.

An interesting detail of this room is that of the arrangement whereby the door can be opened from the bed, the cord that performs this function can be seen in the illustration, running up to the cornice from the bed-head. The original lock is still working on the eight-panelled door.

Here we have a perfect example of the dignified use of wallpaper, for it has been treated in much the same manner as tapestry or fine damask. We find many rooms of this period where the panelling has been made to fit and frame the family tapestries, though in such cases the rooms would naturally be considerably larger and more important than the example shown here.

Another flocked wallpaper of much the same period (1732) and again treated in a similar manner is that at Christchurch mansion at Ipswich. The design is more complicated and considerably bolder, for it papers the walls of a State Bedroom and would therefore seem to be the best that the artists of the day could produce. It will be seen the design is so large that it took one and a half sheets to repeat. The quality of the design dwarfs to a certain extent the fine carving of the overmantel which in itself is an excellent example of the designs for chimney-pieces attributed to Gibbs. The plain marble fire-place and the short wainscot panels give a balance to the room which might otherwise appear over-decorated.

Such fireplaces were rare at this time, especially in the most up-to-date rooms because of the far-felt effects of the published drawings of Inigo Jones (1727) and James Gibbs (1728). These drawings gave measured details of classic ornament as applied to doors, windows, fireplaces and chimney-pieces and within a very

85

Flock Wallpaper
CHRISTCHURCH MANSION IPSWICH
c. 1732

few years of this classic revival hundreds of rooms were re-decorated with the stuccoed embellishments of Palladian architecture.

There is however, another plain marble fireplace in the same house (Christ-church Mansion) which has unusual charm. Here the simple ornament of the

Plaster and Marble Chimney Piece, Painted 'Draperies'

CHRISTCHURCH MANSION

c. 1732

marble structure is confined to the flattened scroll supports. The overmantel is a plaster imitation of drapery arranged in elegant folds the better to set off the very charming bust, (it might be a portrait bust, or an imaginative figure).

This plaster drapery with its minute canopy is painted in scarlet with a gold fringe and tassels and is probably similar to the painted effects so much admired by Cecila Fiennes a few years earlier.

Now of the revivalists of Inigo Jones—one of the best examples in miniature as one could wish to find is that of Ston Easton in Somerset.

87

Details of Designs in Plaster and Carving
used on Frieze and Frame for Grisaille Painting

Ston Easton, Somerset
c. 1740

Designs Carved on
Fireplace and Cupboard
in 'Print Room'

Detail of
Top Moulding

Detail
of Side

STON EASTON
c. 1740

It is not certain at what date the house was 'done up', it could easily have been about 1740. Here we can still see the imposing stucco decorations almost identical in design to those produced by Inigo Jones for his interior at Whitehall and published in Lord Burlington's books. However, at Ston Easton, a reasonably sized country house, the interior architect had to suit his designs to a much smaller setting and the very deep cornice in the salon with its great shells and scrolls picked out by a terra-cotta background is a weighty proposition for the size of the room.

The pedimented doorways and chimney-piece are in complete accord with the original principles, and a Grisaille painting over the fireplace carries out the illusion of classic sculpture.

Grisaille was the term applied to paintings which, in order that they might conform to the demands for classic ornament were carried out in imitation of statuary or relief sculpture. This effect was achieved by painting in oils on canvas in shades of grey, brown or other shadow tones with an appreciative eye to the natural lighting of the room they were to grace.

Mock niches and alcoves with stucco frames frequently contained Grisaille urns or 'statuary'. Some of this type of work was so cleverly carried out that at first glance it can easily be mistaken for what it was intended to represent.

The same idea inspired the wallpaper designers of that time, for many of these wallpapers were hand-painted. Vast schemes based on classic ornament were carried out with amusing results in perspective. That which appears at first glance to be stucco architectural ornament, quite suddenly takes on the strangest of proportions. This is particularly noticeable on staircases where, of course, one is most likely to get sudden changes of vision.

Strips and panels of such ornament were manufactured and supplied by the yard so that those unable to afford the costly plasterwork could quite reasonably carry out similar schemes which might at first glance be mistaken for the actual thing.

An enterprising gentleman by the name of Jackson advertised his ability to produce wallpapers during the 50's in the following manner:—

... 'Antique statues, landscapes after Salvator Rosa, Canaletto, copies of Painters, in short any bird that flies every figure that moves upon the surface of the earth from insect to Human and every Vegetable that springs from the ground. Whatever is of Art or Nature may be introduced into the design ... Saloons in Imitation of Stucco may be done in this manner and staircases in any taste as shall be agreeable ... Thus the person who cannot purchase the statues themselves may have these prints in their places, and may as effectually show his taste and Admiration of the ancient Artists in this manner of fitting up and

90

Detail of Fireplace
COMBE, DEVON
c. 1750

furnishing the Apartments as in the most expensive. 'Tis the choise and not the price which discovers the true taste of the possessor.'

The same artist introduced the first printed coloured paper—something in the nature of a coloured print, and called 'Chiaro oscuro.' These rather brilliant papers, now known as 'Jackson Prints' were extremely crude in colour and followed the 'rococo' styles which were in the 40's and 50's another fashionable departure from classic restrictions.

The 'Rococo' or Venetian style of decoration was based on the Baroque of Italy which followed close upon the heels of the Renaissance. It was a conscious effort to distort and break away from the too familiar and well-balanced aspect of a pure classic ideal. The result as the term 'rococo' implies was a rocky effect with broken pediments and other fragments of architectural significance introduced into a scrolled and foliated whole which was in no wise symmetrical.

The rococo style in England followed immediately after, and was indeed sometimes simultaneous with late Palladian. In the normal way such ornament was executed in stucco or *papier mâché* gilded or coloured, and was included in every type of interior decoration; some of the suggested designs for wall decoration that still exist on paper were altogether overpowering. There were, however, a few delightful examples of 'restrained rococo' and of these a particularly elegant room exists at Combe near Honiton in Devonshire. The decoration is confined to the plaster ceiling, the chimney-piece, and the two doorways, a skirting board with small acanthus leaf moulding runs round the room. Probably the walls were originally hung with silk or a wallpaper, and the original decoration was painted white and gold for traces of this still exist on the ceiling. (See frontispiece.)

Here restraint and elegance are the supreme factors and the whole is extremely happy. This is obviously not the work of a copyist but that of a rare artist.

Fantastic birds perch precariously on fragments of broken architectural form, flowers and fruits, scrolls and urns balance in improbable places, a minute fox beneath the mirror looks up at birds of mammoth proportions, yet the whole flows happily about its business of pleasing decoration.

The carving on the frieze over the doors is also of a rare quality, and combines the features of fine classic proportion and ornament with the same or similar design as that on chimney-piece and ceiling.

Carved Doorway
COMBE, DEVON
c. 1750

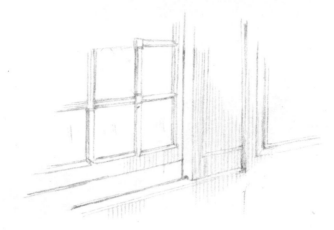

Sliding Shutter
COMPTON BEAUCHAMP, BERKSHIRE
c. 1720

The fitting of a sliding shutter to the sash window with its perfectly square panes of glass is an interesting feature in a boldly panelled room at Compton Beauchamp in Berkshire. Here a sliding panel can be pushed back into a hidden recess behind the panels at the side of the windows.

The shutter is in one piece and runs on a grooved rail with the ease of a perfectly balanced piece of mechanism, but it is the actual weight of the panel and the shaping of the groove and socket that gives it this ease of movement, which has apparently lasted for more than two centuries.

When the shutter-panel is pulled across the window it fits so well into the general scheme of the large panels that line the room that it is practically invisible. This is the type of fine craftsmanship that is so typical of the early years of the eighteenth century.

Shutters of a few years later were made in smaller panels hinged to fold back in the space between the window frame and the panelled wall of the room, and the next instance of a shutter running on a rail does not normally occur until the end of the century when panelling was no longer used.

Compton Beauchamp is one of those lovely houses, Tudor in its original design, built round a stone courtyard. On one side is the old Tudor hall but otherwise the building is early eighteenth century throughout. The dining-room has 'marbled' niches and fine painted panelled walls and most of the windows were converted to the long sash when mullions ceased to be fashionable.

94

Early Eighteenth Century Renovation, Tudor Ceiling

BETTISCOMBE, DORSET

The habit of 'conversion' was rife during the last few years of the 17th century and the early 18th, and many interesting examples of such conversion can be found throughout the length and breadth of the country. At Bettiscombe, Dorset, the old Tudor hall was converted into a well wainscoted room with small sash windows and arcaded columns supporting the ceiling. This ceiling,

95

Small Panelled Room
Early 18th Century
BETTISCOMBE

a fine example of carved cross-beams, was probably too low for the possibility of plaster work being even considered. It was also too low to paint so the 'beams' were painted to match the wainscot and the arcading was fitted into the moulded edge of the beam and a 'keystone' added to give strength to the appearance of the colonnade.

96

Pine Panelling and Carved Stone Columns
WESTWELL, OXFORDSHIRE
c. 1740

Although panelling was no longer the only fashionable wall covering, there were a vast number of houses that were still being panelled but not—as was the invariable case in the late Stuart period—with such large panels nor so bold mouldings.

Panels might be almost any size or shape and we find circular and oval panels with curvated shapes or 'spandrels' filling the space in design. Long narrow panels and panelled columns and chair rails (a moulding to protect the wall from a too hastily pushed back chair).

97

FOUR WALLS ADORNED

Such rooms were often designed to form 'frames' for pictures or mirrors or even small delicate designs on ricepaper or Chinese silk. They were nearly always painted, white and a duck egg green being favourite backgrounds. Now that their original features no longer exist many of these rooms present a curious appearance. In the illustrated example—a delightful little bedroom at Bettiscombe Manor—the size and shape of panels on the fireside wall are all different. Those on the door (leading to the fitted powder closet) are moulded with some seven or eight ridges and a raised panel set inside, the long slit panels beside the door have only a single moulding and do not match. The powder closets in every bedroom are all fitted with their original drawers and cupboards, a tiny set of eight drawers with drop handles for such contemporary necessities as powder, patches, pins, pomatum etc.

We are told that on the site of Westwell in Oxfordshire the remains of a Roman villa were discovered some time during the early years of the Eighteenth Century, and amongst these relics of the past several carved Ionic capitals made their appearance. The immediate architectural value of such treasure inspired the owner to take advantage of the classic revival and construct one room that included these capitals as the chief feature of decoration. This room is panelled in pine, which was probably originally painted. The alcove with its two bowed shelves would undoubtedly have been an original feature and the narrow carved design on the cornice is the only ornament which, though in keeping, does not compete with the fine sculptured capitols to the supporting columns. The rather delicately recessed panels would indicate that the date was somewhere about 1740 when panelling was no longer the main feature of a room and merely served as a simple background for pictures, prints or China-ware. The fashion for panelling was, at this time, quite definitely on the decline for wall-papers and cotton-prints were nearly always to be found covering walls above the low wainscot.

Other interesting features of Westwell introduced at approximately the same date include a marble fireplace with its original hand-bevilled mirror and a very beautiful staircase.

The staircase follows the typical lines of the time and introduces such classic details as dentils, scrolls and a fine Roman Doric column on the bottom stair.

There is abundant evidence that the little house of the eighteenth century could be as well and graciously equipped as the more palatial ones. In fact we find that Pope, at least, was not in favour of the slavish copyists of Palladio . . .

'. . . Yet shall, my Lord, your just four noble rules
Fill half the land with imitating fools;
Who random drawings from your sheets shall take,
And of one beauty many blunders make; . . .'

Marble Fireplace with Mirror

WESTWELL

c. 1740

The really small house was free from such blunders because of its natural limitation of size and the English craftsman pursued his instinct and good taste in equipping such houses with fitted furniture.

In the following illustration is an elegantly proportioned cupboard, one of a pair that stand either side of a plain little fireplace in a tiny room in a cottage

99

WESTWELL
c. 1730

at Bewdley in Worcestershire. These cupboards entirely fill the recess made by
the chimney and are built into the wall forming the main feature of a room
less than 12 ft square. Such little gems of architectural simplicity must still grace

100

One of a Pair of Wall Cupboards

BEWDLEY, WORCESTERSHIRE

c. 1720

many little houses throughout the country—and often, for some obscure reason best known to some past owner—such cupboards have been bricked up or covered with wallpaper and have been re-discovered during constructional alterations at a later date.

This same cottage at Bewdley boasts a lovely oak staircase built in the tradition of the late 17th or early 18th century. It is again a perfect example of simplicity and proportion, and though small it carries all the dignity of the period.

101

BERKSHIRE
c. 1730

Fireplaces with Egg and
Dart and Shell Designs

COLYTON, DEVON

The egg and dart design is one which lends itself, particularly happily, to the design on a framework, and its use during the Elizabethan and Jacobean period did nothing to damp its popularity during the eighteenth century.

In these two examples of fireplaces made, more or less, at the same date, we can compare the similarity of ornament with very different application.

102

The first one is carved in wood and painted and was probably inspired from one of the designs in Gibbs' published works. The other, which is in stone, bears a fleeting resemblance to the Tudor stone fireplaces, but its shape and ornament is quite obviously inspired by the classic revival. Its charming simplicity is a tribute to the 18th century stonemason who carved it,—probably a local country workman, for the fireplace is in an upstairs room in a small house in the village of Colyton in Devon, possibly at one time the main bedroom.

A particularly interesting feature of the decorative works of the late 17th and early 18th century is that of the persistence of the shell motif. The scallop shell appears again and again, making a central figure in practically every design whether it is carried out in wood, stone, stucco, embroidery or any other material.

VI

GEORGE III 1760—1820

When George III embarked on his long reign in 1760 the various styles in decoration that have already been described were all established and although there were a considerable number of houses being built to individual requirements the main theme, on the whole, was still Classic.

It is impossible to deal with this highly cultured phase in our history without simultaneously becoming aware of the great number of gifted craftsmen who left the houses of this country so much richer by their industry and example.

Such names as Chippendale, Sheraton, Hepplewhite, the brothers Adam and their many followers are all intimately concerned with this subject of interior decoration. The many books and folios that were being published—illustrating their various works and explaining how such and such a design was to be carried out—were a boon to the craftsmen throughout the country. The fantastic amount of work attributed to these particular artists is, unfortunately for posterity, quite impossible to verify or believe, but that their designs were copied, with various degrees of success, by both skilled and less skilled workmen, is an undeniable fact. Thus a Hepplewhite chest of drawers today usually means one that can be found illustrated in Hepplewhite's 'Guides' and not necessarily made in his workshop.

When Robert Wood produced illustrated works on the ruins of Palmyra and Baalbek in 1753—57 an interest in Roman grandeur prevailed, to be encouraged further when Robert Adam's 'Diocletian's Palace at Spalato' was published a few years later.

The ease with which a new idea could be thrust upon an educated community with a very vivid interest in anything 'modern' is particularly striking in the latter part of the eighteenth century, and the illustrated book was seldom devoid of such influence. That its individual interpretation was not entirely concerned with architectural construction is abundantly noticeable in the various forms and designs that appeared, inspired by the published drawings but not necessarily relevant to applied architecture; for instance in Chippendale's 'Gentleman & Cabinet Makers' Directory' published in 1754 designs and borders appear for

104

paper-hangings. These 'designs' consist of such things as urns and swags, classic pictures and the smaller motifs employed in classic design. They were meant to be cut out and stuck on to a wall to give a classic flavour to the room they graced. As the paper-hanger was often also the artist who designed and printed his own papers, we may assume that such designs and others like them were copied and carried out throughout the country.

The room illustrated overleaf is an amusing departure from what had originally been intended. When Ston Eaton was built the cupboards, cornice and fireplace of this little room were designed to carry out the general scheme used in the whole house—that of a Palladian building in the Inigo Jones tradition. The room was, however, re-decorated at some time towards the close of the century with the prints, swags, urns and 'miniatures' already mentioned, that appeared in book form ready to hand for the home decorator.

The present owner holds a theory—handed down in the family—that the decoration of this particular room was the careful work of two aunts. These ladies may possibly have been great-aunts or even great-great-aunts. It is, of course, almost impossible to date the 'prints' because they nearly all depict scenes and figures of the past, and mostly show the nude and draped figure in Heroic classic style. There is however, one exception which shows the inside of a prison and women prisoners wearing the clothes of the 1780's or 90's. This was in all probability a print from some incident connected with the French Revolution.

The walls here were once a brilliant turquoise blue, the ornament round the window is still in its original glory of gold and turquoise, the prints, an assortment of mezzotints of varying sizes, are arranged with little swags and streamers of flowers and fruits between, giving an illusion of hanging from an imaginary series of lines. At the top of the low wainscot, urns are arranged at intervals.

There is little doubt that the finely proportioned rooms and elegant decorations which are most keenly associated with the second half of the eighteenth century are those stamped with the indelible 'Adam' touch. Theirs was the last fine attempt in the classic style as inspired by visits to Dalmatia. Ornament was fine and delicate, adapting such motifs as the urn, bell-like swag, and marigold, and introducing medallions in both plasterwork and frieze paintings.

As the carvings of Grinling Gibbons had helped Sir Christopher Wren to establish a fine style of interior decoration—so did Angelica Kauffman contribute to the effect of the Adam's interior.

Angelica Kauffman, a Swiss artist best known for her silhouette paintings and classic medallions, lived in England for many years and applied herself

105

Corner of Print Decorated Room
STON EASTON, SOMERSET
c. 1795

to the nude and draped figure decorations so fashionable towards the end of the century. It was a period when women were accepted for their intellectual and artistic abilities, and there was no particular prejudice against women practising the arts, as there was during the Victorian era.

Although there probably were no small houses actually decorated by Angelica Kauffman's hand, her example was imitated throughout the country, and ladies of all stations expressed their artistic inclinations in the decoration of their homes.

Farrington's Diary (1797) tells us that Frogmore was decorated in one room by the Princess Royal with thirty-six drawings in pen and ink besides ornaments on chair covers etc., and that the Princess Elizabeth had decorated a long narrow room with painted flowers and subjects of children etc. cut out in paper. Possibly the example of Angelica Kauffman's success did much to stimulate a genuine interest in interior decoration.

Side by side with the fine Adam rooms with their beautifully carved marble fireplaces and refined stucco ornament, we find the first 'Holy Gloom' of the Gothic Revival. This was a phase—far-reaching in its example—which first appeared in Horace Walpole's famous building at Strawberry Hill, (started in 1753 and finished in 1778). Walpole in his search for that which was as far removed from the 'outmoded' classic as possible, wanted his new wallpapers painted with a Gothic design. In order to get the real atmosphere he desired, his artist was instructed to visit Durham Cathedral for inspiration, and there to make drawings of the cathedral aisles and 'holy glooms.' The whole scheme of decoration at Strawberry Hill was a conscious effort to establish a new order for interior decoration, and there is no doubt that the example set by Walpole in the eighteenth century set the pace for the Romantic Age of the early nineteenth.

Even whilst Adam designs were being carried out there were a vast number of intellectuals who condemned his 'filigree' ornament and praised the exponents of the Gothic Revival.

Apart from the Gothic wallpapers, the smaller house was rarely influenced by this particular phase until about 1800 when 'Gothic' doors and windows appeared in the thatched cottage and seaside villa, and cluster columns took the place of the classic pilaster.

Panelling had practically disappeared before George III came to the throne, its use as a wall-covering being entirely superseded by wallpapers and materials. Plastered walls were sometimes divided into large 'panels' by a plaster rib and small ornaments in the classic style. The papered walls were often decorated with the popular sporting print, a series of engravings, a set of family silhouettes. All these details can be clearly seen in the 'Conversation Pieces' of the time.

The influence of the Orient was more apparent as the century progressed, and lacquered furniture, China silks and carpets, were as much in use as the beautiful furnishings made by the English craftsmen of the period.

Of these furnishings a variety of forms made their appearance in the later years of the eighteenth century and their ornament and design have not been improved upon since. The English cabinet-maker had reached a stage of perfection in his work that can never be truly imitated by factory-made furniture of a later date. Chairs, tables, bookcases, clocks, settees, daybeds, sofas, desks, cupboards and chests, and the most comfortable armchair of all, the 'wingback', were not the only items of furniture that received special attention from the artist; there were a hundred and one ornaments and foibles of the time cherished by the fashionable world that are out of place today—such as wigstands, knife-bozes, sconces, torchieres, wine-boxes, fire screens etc.—each useful in its original setting and still a thing of beauty.

Though many still favoured the four-poster bed, of some fine imported wood, mostly mahogany, there were any amount of curious experiments in shape and construction as well as material. The draped top still continued in favour but the bottom of the bed had changed its shape. Towards the end of the century we find examples in various furniture catalogues of the most fantastic beds—oval and circular, and even a pair of twin beds with the same canopy 'for summer use' illustrated in Sheraton's 'Drawing Book'.

So varied were the styles of furnishings that it is impossible to do more than refer the interested reader to the books that give their original design.

From 1760 to 1800 the craze for the 'pastoral' or rustic still engaged the attention of a great majority and a variety of quaint conceits appeared in and around the home to add charm and character to the property. This was an age when the wonders of clockwork and other machinery were manifold, the musical-box, the singing bird, the dancing peasants, were all elegant entertainments. Pagodas, Moorish summer-houses and ornamental lakes with gondolas and Chinese junks were frequently peopled by mechanised figures.

Curtains, hangings and soft furnishings generally, changed considerably during this period and this was due to the old ways of spinning and weaving being greatly improved by such things as Hargreaves' 'Spinning Jenny' (1767), Crompton's 'mule' (1775), and Cartwright's loom (1787). Each invention lessened the time and labour that had previously been spent in the manufacture of materials.

By 1775 the fashion for pattern in furnishing materials and curtains was beginning to die out. Stripes were the order of the day, and though clothes still carried a rich variety of floral embroideries and painted bouquets the sofa

RAMSBURY, WILTSHIRE

Adam Fireplace, Iron Circular Grate
SADBOROW, DORSET
c. 1775

and couch, arm-chair and curtain, all displayed a stripe in some form or other. Frequently such stripes were woven only, changing the surface of the material like a damask.

From a vast selection of fine Adam interiors (and many others claimed to be the work of the Adam brothers), one particularly gracious house in Dorset, that of Sadborow, has claimed my attention, for, apart from one large room re-decorated in the early 19th century, the house retains most of the original features of 1775, the year it was completed. Doorways and fireplaces are in the Adam tradition and a fine circular wrought iron staircase with arches leading to the rooms upstairs gives dignity to the entrance hall.

109

Detail of Decoration

SADBOROW
c. 1775

One downstairs room is a particularly fine example of workmanship even to the circular iron grate. The fireplace is made of wood decorated with gesso and the iron grate fits snugly into the perfect square of the opening. The grate is designed with side panels carrying the urn and 'S' design with the oval marigold appearing at the base and again in the four corners outside the circular fire

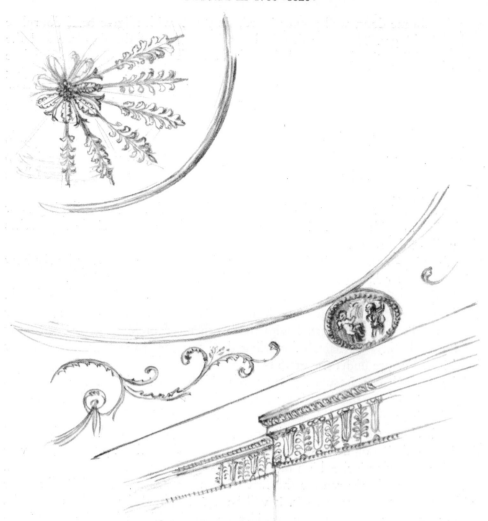

Corner of Adam Ceiling
SADBOROW
c. 1775

opening; a tiny ribbon design runs round this opening. The frieze beneath the
mantelpiece is decorated with gesso swags and the flattened urn with curved
handles in the centre panel. Dentils appear under the cornice of the mantelshelf.
In all probability this fireplace was painted in contrasting colours as has recently
been done with the decoration over the doorway of the same room. It is a

111

very handsome door, well proportioned, six panels with filigree brass doorplate and plain hinges. The same dentilled cornice as that of the fireplace and the same mouldings in the recessed door frame as that surrounding the fireplace itself are used again, but the frieze is quite different. The bell chain hanging from the acanthus is the same design as that of the swags on the fireplace. The cornice that joins the ceiling to the walls of the room repeats the design of that over the door.

The plasterwork of the ceiling is executed with the greatest delicacy—so fine is the work that had the windows not been so tall and given the ceiling so much light it would be extremely difficult to trace the fine swirling lines of the corner designs.

The centrepiece is arranged with radiating heads of corn and little plaques or medallions; cupids representing the arts appear whenever the circle approaches the walls of the room.

A drawing-room upstairs boasts an even finer fireplace and very lovely bow windows, but otherwise the room is devoid of contemporary detail.

The fireplace is marble with the pattern inlaid in contrasting shades of pink, black and grey marble. Here the iron grate is an open one with a half circle under the bars; it is decorated with the 'Anthemon' or honeysuckle ornament on the fireback, and chains of swirling dots and the 'patera' or single flower head in the centre under the grate bars.

The mantelpiece is supported by beautifully proportioned Ionic pilasters with the 'vase' on the top. Very lovely, almost transparent marble, has been used for these pilasters which are practically dead white, the same as that used for the background of the inlaid design running along the top. The finely carved detail swag design on the vase gives it the elegance of the finest porcelain, the vase itself is only a few inches high but there is not a faulty line or detail anywhere.

In this example we can see the first wide mantelshelf—a flat slab of marble without a cornice to support it. It will be noted that all the previous examples show that that which we now consider a mantelshelf was but the natural top of an ornamental cornice and frieze—it was not originally conceived as a bracket to hold vases and clocks which has since proved its use.

The influence of sport on society in the second half of the eighteenth century has already been remarked in the fashion for sporting prints and paintings used to decorate the walls of rooms. Calico prints and wallpapers were also decorated with hunting scenes, horse racing, cock-fighting; or shooting and fishing groups, but the actual introduction of the sporting motif as a design for a fireplace is not so common. There is however, a very fine example of a 'shooting' fireplace at Grange in Devonshire.

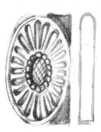

Detail of
'Marigold'

Detail of
Urn and
Ionic Capital

Marble Fireplace with Iron Grate
SADBOROW
c. 1775

Detail of Carving
under Mantlepiece

GRANGE, BROADHEMBURY
c. 1770

This particular room was obviously 'done up' some time between 1770 and 1780. The ceiling plastered with a fine circular design after the Adams' style and a new fireplace introduced where in all probability the plaster one with the angels (see p. 43) or one similar in design had originally been.

114

This 'new' fireplace is of finely carved wood on a marble back, painted after the fashionable manner to match the wainscot.

The carved 'cornice' follows the traditional classic form of ornament and the oval marigold appears on either side of the frieze, otherwise the design is singularly original. Two pointers — one actually 'pointing' and the other crouched,—appear either side of the centre panel where a brace of pheasant lie in a realistic heap. The side panels are decorated with guns each differing slightly and one complete with powder bag. The whole is an extremely happy combination of classic ornament with the very ordinary impedimenta of the sportsman of the eighteenth century. The craftsman employed, although familiar with the fashionable demands for classic exactitude, has preferred to use his imagination rather than copy too closely the instruments of a bygone civilization when those of his own could make a perfectly good design and a much more original display.

There are, of course, many more adaptations of contemporary details to be found generally in the designs of the late Georgian time; these appear quite often in plaster ceilings and in many instances we can see the artist's desire to express the personal interests of the people for whom he is decorating. Even more frequently do we find the various forms of art or sport expressed in medallions where cherubs or fat babies are introduced carrying out some form of work (for which they are too obviously unsuitable) equipped with the tools of their supposed trade.

In the year 1792 Lord Macartney of Coutts Bank and a few of his especial friends had hand-painted Chinese wallpapers sent from China to decorate their homes. The example now at Coutts Bank is famous and has been admired and discussed for 150 years, but there are still a number of others similar in design to be 'discovered' in other houses in England. At Ramsbury near Marlborough— a lovely house that boasts other Chinese papers as well—there is a little study with a full scenic wallpaper in nearly perfect condition. At the base of the design is a rocky foreground which rises to a sea full of scattered islands, boats and bridges, with high pinnacled mountains, and clouds in the background. The colours are soft and delicate, green and an apricot colour predominating. At the top and bottom of the paper is a little 'border' which follows the line round the fireplace and over the doors. The paper was designed to fill this particular room for where the door and fireplace occur the foreground rises and adjusts itself to the space it has to fill. This paper came to England on the same ship as that of Lord Macartney's and was probably 'hung' within the year.

Panels of a similar design, but including more figures, are at Bridehead in Dorset. Probably at some time these panels were part of a whole room or they

115

might have been a 'copy.' The most interesting feature of such design is that even where a space is the same there is virtually no repeat, each strip of paper is entirely different from its neighbour yet they fit together so beautifully that it is extremely difficult to see where they join. It seems a great pity that within a few short years wallpaper printing put an end to the importation of the hand-painted designs—except in very special cases. (Machine printing came into general use in 1799).

When we realise, however, the changing fashions in the new machine printed wallpapers it is easy to see that rooms ceased to be built and decorated to last. Each succeeding owner could with economy and despatch entirely alter the whole house to his liking. A contemporary advertisement for wallpapers claimed that 'Rooms with bare walls could be given the beauty, elegance and convenience of a well stuccoed apartment'.

During the twenty years this book covers after the invention of machine printing, the variety of such papers was practically unlimited. Papers in large panels with scenery were a special delight. Trellised papers with flowers and animals, papers resembling tiles, Egyptian and Grecian designs, Gothic, Indian, Chinese. Everything in fact except the busy little repeating patterns with which the succeeding generations had been all too familiar.

Flocked wallpapers were in use right through the eighteenth century, but where in the earliest examples the background was a beige or off-white, the later design shows a darker background. In other rooms at Bridehead there are quite a collection of such papers, some of them of Victorian design. The one shown here is believed to be that of about 1795 for the room has not been 'done up' since that date. The paper is held in position with a gilt edging which covers the edges and corners throughout. This edging is still very bright and has probably been re-gilded. The paper is very thick and the flocking is done in gold on a blue ground and looks very much like velvet. This paper, unlike the earlier examples at Chillington and Ipswich, was obviously supplied in 'rolls' and not small sheets, for there is no visible 'join' in the upright sheets although the room is very high.

The fireplace of marble has a polished iron grate, and was probably designed by a follower of the Adam Brothers. Such iron grates are a particular feature of the late 18th century and very beautiful most of them are. The general idea is that they are 'steel' but this is a mistake. They are the finest type of beaten ironwork made before the introduction of 'cast' iron. When once thoroughly polished they should keep their very brilliant lustre.

The smaller house built at this time included the seaside house or the country cottage built by the nouveau-riche for the fashionable 'change of air'. Sea

116

Detail of Gilt
Edging

Detail of
Supporting
Capitol on
Fireplace

Flocked Wallpaper in Blue and Gold
BRIDEHEAD, DORSET
c. 1795

Detail of Carved
Centre Decoration

Marble Fireplace and Window with Running Shutter
ROUGEMONT HOUSE, EXETER
c. 1820

bathing and the benefits to be derived from the sea breezes were beginning to over-shadow the popularity of the visit to the Baths and taking the waters at the famous watering places. It is therefore at places like Weymouth, Brighton, and Sidmouth that we find the best examples of the true Regency House— one that was built between 1810 and 1820, with its Trafalgar Balconies, French windows and distinctly 'Gothic' atmosphere. There are many charming houses with long sash windows and beautifully fitted mahogany doors which have for a great many years been known as 'Regency' Houses but in truth they are earlier and quite definitely still the work of the 18th century craftsman.

Many such craftsmen did quite often carry on their own family tradition, regardless of the changing shape of things around them, and there are many isolated examples of fine workmanship in the 18th century style to be found half buried in the 'fuss' of the 19th. We also find a few attractive examples where the craftsman is more interested in doing something different and individual than following the accepted formula of his time.

An interesting example of the desire to be 'different' is that of the fireplace-window at Rougemont House in Exeter.

This house, built in 1820, retains little detail in its original form, although from the outside it presents an imposing facade with Trafalgar Balcony and long bowed sash windows. The hall is supported with Roman Doric columns and there are one or two plain marble fireplaces with little or no ornament.

It is difficult to imagine how it was originally decorated but the rooms are finely proportioned and well lit, and there is nothing Gothic about them.

The fireplace in this particular room is made from a grey-blue marble, and its 'mantelshelf', which is also the window-sill has shutters running on a little bowed 'railway-line' to meet in the middle.

There are two chimneys, running up either side of the window and, apparently, fires can still be lit and enjoyed without undue smoke.

The fireplace itself is vaguely classic for it uses forms of acanthus leaf designs, but the whole shape is something entirely original and unexpected as it is bowed and the two sides face outward at an unusual angle.

The hearth follows this curious line and the original fender must have been especially constructed. As a whole it is both original and solidly constructional, but at the same time we can see the 'shape of things to come'. Within a very few years the same or similar shapes, less well balanced, were being produced in cast-iron by the factories and the handmade varieties became scarcer and scarcer.

This little Gothic house at Sidmouth with its bow windows and coloured glass still retains a certain quality and charm reminiscent of Jane Austin and Mary Russell Mitford. The desire to carry out the true Gothic style had not, so far, penetrated to the 'decorated' stage and apart from the use of the Tudor arch and Early English columns, there is little indication of the ponderous and depressing influence that eventually became part and parcel of the Gothic Revival. It can be seen in the illustration that the curve of the ceiling in the window alcove gave shape to the outside form, which so often enhanced the houses on the sea fronts and at the same time carried out the curious 'tent' or 'pavilion' shapes, so particularly fashionable during the Regency. The whole house is constructionally as it must have been 130 years ago. The narrow entrance hall has Gothic doors opening from it and cluster columns at the bottom of the staircase; coloured glass has been used in most of the windows, and iron railings and balconies decorate the front of the house. The walls are devoid of stucco design, so that in all probability wallpapers were originally included. The paint has unfortunately been too heavily applied and some of the finer work, such as the mouldings on the columns, is partially obliterated. Panelling only appears in the window alcove, its use as a practical covering for an outside wall being obvious rather than ornamental. This example of interior decoration virtually brings to an end the period under review for we have come to a stage in our history when craftsmanship ceased to play an individual part in any scheme of decoration.

The hand-painted wallpaper was rare and a limited variety of machine-printed papers had already come onto the market. The designs of such papers displayed an interest in the immediate contemporary occurrences, such as the Battle of the Nile and the 'Empire' styles of Napoleonic France. 'Egyptian' wallpaper was so much used during the first few years after its original printing that by 1812 it was only to be found in hotels and boardinghouses.

With the coming of the machine-age the whole pace of life had been speeded up. Ideas no longer filtered gently through the country to be absorbed ten or twenty years later in the smaller country towns. Communication and better roads made the whole of England more easily accessible and there was no reason why a style seen in London, Bristol or Birmingham should not be copied within a very few weeks of its origin in the more remote towns and villages.

Everything seen and admired could now with very little trouble and expense be reproduced. Eighteenth century taste with its overwhelming passion for imitation had developed into the perfect market for the nineteenth century manufacturer. The stage was now set for the entrance of the professional Interior Decorator and he made his debut appropriately, in an avalanche of fringed draperies, gorgeous lighting effects and a mass of oriental 'Props'. As this gentleman's livelihood was dependant on his ability to make yesterday's fashion an unforgivable offence to the Man of Taste, the mere walls of a room became the background for the paperhanger's repertoire and the setting for the rapidly changing scene.

120

BEACH HOUSE, SIDMOUTH